MODERN **GRILL PAN** COOKING

MODERN **GRILL PAN** COOKING

BY GINA STEER

CB

CONTEMPORARY BOOKS

A QUINTET BOOK

This book was conceived, designed, and produced by
Quintet Publishing Limited
6 Blundell Street
London N7 9BH
England

Project Editor: Carine Tracanelli
Editor: Anna Bennett
Designer: Deep Design
Photographer: Ian Garlick
Food Stylist: Kathryn Hawkins

Creative Director: Richard Dewing
Publisher: Oliver Salzmann

Typeset in Great Britain
by Central Southern Typesetters, Eastbourne
Manufactured in Hong Kong
by Regent Publishing Services Limited

Published by Contemporary Books
A division of NTC/Contemporary Publishing Group, Inc.
4255 West Touhy Avenue
Lincolnwood (Chicago), Illinois 60712-1975 U.S.A.
Copyright © 2000 by Quintet Publishing Limited
All rights reserved. No part of this book may be reproduced,
stored in a retrieval system, or transmitted in any form
or by any means, electronic, mechanical, photocopying,
recording, or otherwise, without the prior written permission
of NTC/Contemporary Publishing Group, Inc.
Printed in China by Leefung-Asco Printers Trading Limited
International Standard Book Number: 0-8092-9663-2
00 01 02 03 04 05   19 18 17 16 15 14 13 12 11 10 9 8 7 6 5 4 3 2 1

Library of Congress Cataloging-in-Publication Data

Steer, Gina.
    Modern grill pan cooking : 100 innovative recipes for perfect results / Gina Steer.
        p. cm.
ISBN 0-8092-9663-2
    1. Barbecue cookery. 2. Grill pans. I. Title.

TX840.B3 S733 2000
641.7′6--dc21
                                                    00-35853

AUTHOR'S ACKNOWLEDGMENTS

I would like to thank Kim Clitter for all her invaluable help in the testing of the recipes in this book. Plus John, my husband who as
ever was my main guinea pig, not forgetting the rest of my family and friends who also helped in the tasting of all the recipes.
Special thanks to Le Creuset for providing us with their excellent grill pans for use in the testing of the recipes and photography.

Some recipes in this book use raw eggs. Because of the slight risk of salmonella, raw eggs should not be served
to the very young, the ill or the elderly, or to pregnant women.

CONTENTS

INTRODUCTION

Why bother with a grill pan when an ordinary skillet will work just as well? The answer is that cooking with a grill pan is a totally different experience. Not only is it a very effective way of reducing your fat intake (you only need a minimum amount of oil or butter to cook your food), but it also speeds up the cooking time quite considerably, as well as producing sensational-looking results.

Using a ridged grill pan gives an indoor-barbecue look to your food with attractive markings across the food. It will also enable you to cook mouthwatering, imaginative dishes that combine ingredients from both East and West, producing light, fresh meals that will appeal to all.

CHOOSING YOUR GRILL PAN

Using a grill pan is easy providing you follow a few simple guidelines. It is a question of personal preference whether you choose a nonstick pan or heavy cast-iron pan. All you would normally need when cooking in either pan is a fine spray of oil, used when you first begin to heat your grill pan.

When choosing your grill pan, buy the best you can afford. The heavier the pan, the better the result, because the pan needs to withstand high temperatures and a light pan may buckle and distort after a few uses. Grill pans look like skillets, have distinctive ridges across the surface, and come in all shapes and sizes, round, square, or oblong. There is also an attractive variety of high-quality grill pans in a range of awe-inspiring colors designed to combine with the color scheme of your kitchen and other pans. The design of the pans is extremely clever, because the ridges on the surface allow the excess fat to flow out of the food during cooking and most pans have a lip at the side to enable you to pour off any excess fat, thus providing a healthy meal.

Ensure when choosing your pan you buy one that will suit your family size and lifestyle. After using your grill pan a few times you will be so impressed with the results that you will be rushing out to purchase a second pan.

COOKING WITH A GRILL PAN

Always read the manufacturer's instructions before you begin to cook with your grill pan, and follow any special guidelines that are recommended. You will be amazed at how easy cooking in a grill pan can be. The food is quickly sealed on both sides, ensuring that all the flavor is encased. Food is more tender and succulent and by marinating first you can impart wonderful flavors that will be retained throughout the cooking process. It is important that the food is sealed completely on one side before turning over and sealing the other side, otherwise the food may stick during cooking. As soon as the food is completely sealed, the heat can then be lowered for the rest of the cooking time. This is very important with foods that take a little while to cook, otherwise the outside of the food will burn.

CARING FOR YOUR PAN

Before using your grill pan for the first time you should wash it in hot soapy water, dry it thoroughly, then oil it very lightly with vegetable oil. Then every time you use your pan, either lightly brush or spray with oil and preheat it on a moderate heat for about 2 to 4 minutes, depending on the weight of the pan, before you start to cook or, if preferred, simply heat the pan until hot and add the food to be cooked. It is recommended to spray the pan with oil as it helps prevent the food from burning if the pan is too hot. It also prevents tender meats from tearing. If using a cast-iron grill pan you should not cook on a high heat at all because these pans retain their heat for a considerable length of time. To begin with, test the heat temperature in your pan by sprinkling a few drops of cold water into the pan. If it sizzles and evaporates immediately the pan is ready for use. Oven mitts are always essential items to have as the handle can get hot. Use wooden implements, or sturdy plastic, not metal, so the surface cannot be scratched or damaged in any way.

After use, never plunge the grill pan into cold water because this may warp your pan. Do not plunge it into hot water or immediately fill it with very hot water because this will cause spitting and could damage the surface. Always allow the pan to cool, then immerse in hot soapy water and leave for a while. The pan will then clean up very easily. If any food particles are left after soaking, use a nylon scourer or brush, never a metal cleaner, which would scratch and damage the surface. Rinse and dry thoroughly then store in a dry cupboard. Do not leave the pan to drain. Some people lightly oil their pan after drying, but it is not necessary to do so.

COOKING TECHNIQUES

Food that has been marinated needs to be drained well before being placed in the pan. If a recipe calls for the marinade to be added to the pan, always do this at the end of cooking because it is being used to impart flavor. If a recipe specifies a yogurt marinade, drain well and ensure that the grill pan is not overhot. The temperature of the pan in this case needs to be moderate. With yogurt-based recipes, a little extra oil is usually required to ensure that the food does not char and burn on the outside before the inside is cooked.

I have used sunflower oil in many of the recipes because its light flavor will not interfere with the other flavors in the recipe. Olive oil is also fine, but do not use extra-virgin olive oil, because its fine, delicate, and distinctive flavor is wasted in cooking and works much better in dressings and mayonnaise.

I have included a few desserts in the book, with which I have used a little butter (always use sweet butter). Take great care because the heat of the grill pan when hot will burn butter very easily. If preferred, oil can be used instead of the butter in these recipes.

INGREDIENTS

Because of the principles of cooking in a grill pan, it is important that you use top-quality foods that only require minimal cooking times. Grill pans are not suitable for cooking meats that require long slow cooking in order to tenderize the food.

Marinades serve two purposes in grill-pan cooking. The flavors used in the marinade will be reflected in the finished dish, plus marinades also help to tenderize food making it quicker to cook.

Fresh herbs are used extensively throughout the book, to impart a fresh flavor as well as piquancy and color. Use fresh herbs wherever possible because the flavor is far superior to dried. If fresh herbs are not available, try to use freeze-dried or frozen herbs and do ensure that you store them correctly. If using dried herbs, store in a cool dark cupboard, do not expose them to the light, and use as quickly as possible. Use half quantities of dried herbs to fresh.

Chillies, garlic, shallots, and onions also play an important part in the flavoring of many dishes. These as well as other fresh ingredients should be as fresh as possible and prepared as required in order to preserve their flavor and intensity. If a marinade includes small pieces of chopped garlic, onion, chili, and shallots, brush these off before cooking because they may burn during the cooking process.

Once you have become used to your grill pan, I can assure you that you will wonder how you ever managed without one. I certainly do and I hope that you will derive as much pleasure from cooking with your grill pan as I have from writing this book.

FISH &
SHELLFISH

RED MULLET WITH PLUM SAUCE

THIS RECIPE WORKS WELL WITH ANY SMALL WHOLE FISH SO LONG AS THEY ARE NOT TOO BONY. LEAVE THE HEADS ON OR REMOVE THEM, ACCORDING TO PERSONAL PREFERENCE.

Rinse the fish and pat dry. Mix the cinnamon, garlic, and seasoning together and sprinkle into the fish cavities. Place in a shallow dish and pour over the lemon juice and oil. Cover lightly and leave to marinate in the refrigerator for at least 30 minutes. Spoon the marinade over occasionally.

Meanwhile make the plum sauce by placing all the ingredients for the sauce in a small pan with 2 tablespoons of water and simmer uncovered for 15 minutes or until a thick saucelike consistency is reached.

Lightly brush or spray your pan with oil then place on a moderate heat until hot. Drain the fish, reserving 2 tablespoons of the marinade. Cook the fish for 4 minutes on each side or until done, adding the marinade halfway through the cooking time.

Garnish the fish with parsley and serve with the sauce, salad, new potatoes, or freshly cooked egg noodles.

Serves **4**
Preparation time
   10 minutes plus 30 minutes marinating time
Cooking time **8 minutes for the fish, 15 minutes for the sauce**

Four 8- to 10-oz red mullet, cleaned and descaled
1 tsp ground cinnamon
2 garlic cloves, peeled and crushed
Salt and freshly ground black pepper
6 Tbsp lemon juice
2 Tbsp sunflower oil

FOR THE PLUM SAUCE

1 lb fresh plums, rinsed and pitted
2 Tbsp light soft brown sugar
2 garlic cloves, peeled and crushed
1 Tbsp lemon zest
1 tsp ground cinnamon

TO GARNISH

Chopped parsley

TO SERVE

Tossed green salad and new potatoes, or freshly cooked egg noodles

CHARGRILLED SALMON

THIS ATTRACTIVE AND DELICIOUS RECIPE FOR SALMON IS BOTH
QUICK AND EASY, AND MAKES AN IDEAL CHOICE FOR A DINNER
PARTY MEAL IF YOU ARE IN A HURRY.

Serves **4**
Preparation time **5 to 8 minutes plus**
   30 minutes marinating time
Cooking time **6 to 8 minutes for the**
   salmon, 4 minutes for the spinach

Four 5-oz salmon fillet pieces
Salt and freshly ground black pepper
3 Tbsp grated lemon zest
2 Tbsp lemon juice
4 Tbsp olive oil
2 garlic cloves, peeled and crushed

1 to 2 red serrano chillies, seeded and
   sliced
1½ lb fresh spinach
4 shallots, peeled and cut into thin
   wedges
2 Tbsp toasted pine nuts

TO GARNISH
Red chili strips

TO SERVE
Sautéed potatoes

Wipe the salmon and place in a shallow dish. Mix together the seasoning,
2 tablespoons of lemon zest, lemon juice, oil, garlic, and chillies and pour over
the fish. Cover lightly and leave in the refrigerator for at least 30 minutes,
spooning the marinade occasionally over the fish.

Meanwhile thoroughly wash the spinach, discarding any tough stems. Drain well.

Lightly brush or spray your grill pan with oil then place on a moderate heat until
hot. Drain the salmon, reserving the marinade, and cook the salmon on both
sides for 3 to 4 minutes or until done. Add 2 tablespoons of the marinade halfway
through the cooking time.

Heat a wok or large pan and add 2 tablespoons of the reserved marinade. Stir-fry
the shallots for 1 minute then add the spinach and continue to stir-fry for 2 minutes
then sprinkle in the pine nuts. Heat for 30 seconds then arrange on four individual
plates, top with the salmon, skin-side up if liked, scatter with the remaining lemon
zest and chili strips, and serve with the sautéed potatoes.

Chargrilled Salmon

SARDINES WITH
ORANGE AND ROSEMARY

MAKE SURE YOUR SARDINES ARE REALLY FRESH WHEN BUYING.
THEY SHOULD HAVE BRIGHT CLEAR EYES AND THE SKIN SHOULD
BE SHINY, FEEL FIRM TO THE TOUCH, AND SMELL OF THE SEA.

Serves **4**
Preparation time **6 minutes plus
  2 hours marinating time**
Cooking time **4 to 6 minutes**

8 fresh sardines, cleaned
Salt and freshly ground black
  pepper
4 Tbsp orange juice
3 Tbsp olive oil
4 to 6 shallots, peeled and cut into
  thin wedges
2 Tbsp orange zest
Few sprigs fresh rosemary

TO GARNISH
**Fresh rosemary sprigs and
  orange wedges**

Lightly rinse the sardines and pat dry. Season and place in a shallow dish.
Mix the orange juice and oil together and pour over the sardines. Scatter with
the shallots and orange zest. Tear the rosemary into small sprigs then scatter
over the sardines. Cover lightly and leave in the refrigerator for at least 2 hours.
Turn the sardines over halfway through.

Lightly brush or spray your grill pan with oil then place on a moderate heat
until hot. Drain the sardines and cook in the heated pan for 2 to 3 minutes on
each side or until done.

Serve garnished with fresh rosemary sprigs and orange wedges.

SEARED SEAFOOD KABOBS

WHEN MAKING THESE DELICIOUS KABOBS, MAKE SURE TO USE FIRM-FLESHED FISH THAT WILL NOT BREAK UP DURING COOKING.

Combine all the ingredients for the dip, mix well, cover, and leave for at least 30 minutes to allow the flavors to develop.

Lightly rinse the fish, cut into bite-size cubes, and place in a shallow dish. Mix together the garlic, two chopped lemon grass stalks, the ginger, lime juice, and oil and pour over the fish. Cover lightly and leave in the refrigerator for at least 30 minutes. Spoon the marinade occasionally over the fish.

Lightly brush or spray your grill pan with oil then place on a moderate heat until hot. Drain the fish, reserving the marinade, then either skewer alternate pieces of fish onto the lemon grass stalks, if using, or eight small wooden skewers. To skewer the lemon grass stalks more easily, pierce the pieces of fish making a hole first with a skewer. The stalks will slide in easily. Cook in the grill pan, brushing with a little of the marinade as necessary, for 5 minutes or until done, turning once.

Serve with the prepared dip, rice, warm pita bread, and the Oriental Salad.

Serves **4**

Preparation time **8 to 10** minutes plus 30 minutes marinating time

Cooking time **5 minutes**

FOR THE DIP

⅔ cup low-fat, plain yogurt

One 2-in piece cucumber, peeled and diced fine

2 Tbsp chopped fresh cilantro

1 Tbsp chopped fresh flat-leaf parsley

1 tsp lime zest

FOR THE FISH

1 lb assorted fish fillets such as angler fish, salmon, raw jumbo shrimp, snapper

2 garlic cloves, peeled and crushed

2 stalks lemon grass, outer leaves removed and chopped

2 Tbsp grated fresh ginger

3 Tbsp lime juice

5 Tbsp olive oil

TO SERVE

Steamed rice, warm pita bread, and Oriental Salad
(see page 102)

TROUT WITH TOMATO
AND ONION MARMALADE

PREPARE THE MARMALADE AHEAD OF TIME SO THAT IF TIME IS SHORT, IT WILL NOT BE LONG BEFORE YOU ARE SERVING UP THIS DELICIOUS DISH.

Heat the oil in a small pan and gently sauté the onion and garlic for 5 minutes then add the tomatoes and sugar. Bring to a boil then reduce the heat and simmer uncovered for 15 minutes or until a thick consistency is reached. Stir in the parsley and keep warm.

Lightly rinse the trout fillets and pat dry. Sprinkle with seasoning to taste, chillies, and lime zest.

Rinse the chard or spinach leaves, discarding any tough stems. Blanch for 1 minute in boiling water, drain, and pat dry. Use to wrap round the trout fillets.

Lightly brush or spray your grill pan with oil then place on a moderate heat until hot. Add the fillets to the pan and cook on both sides for 2 to 3 minutes or until the chard or spinach is lightly charred and the trout is done.

Garnish with lime wedges and serve with fries and ratatouille.

Serves **4**
Preparation time
   10 to 12 minutes
Cooking time **5 to 7 minutes**
   for the fish, 15 minutes for
   the Marmalade

FOR THE MARMALADE
1 Tbsp oil
1 small onion, peeled and
   chopped fine
2 garlic cloves, peeled and
   chopped fine
10 oz ripe tomatoes, skinned
1 Tbsp dark brown sugar, or to
   taste
1 Tbsp chopped fresh parsley

FOR THE FISH
8 small trout fillets, skinned
Salt and freshly ground black
   pepper
1 tsp crushed dried chillies
1 Tbsp grated lime zest
8 to 16 large fresh chard or
   spinach leaves

TO GARNISH
Lime wedges

TO SERVE
Large fries and ratatouille

SEAFOOD TIKKA KABOBS

THESE KABOBS REQUIRE A YOGURT-BASED MARINADE. WHEN
READY TO COOK, DRAIN THE FISH WELL. USE WOODEN SKEWERS.
MAKE SURE THAT EACH SIDE IS SEALED WELL BEFORE TURNING.

Serves **4**
Preparation time **8 to 10 minutes plus
30 minutes marinating time**
Cooking time **12 minutes for the rice,
6 to 8 minutes for the kabobs**

FOR THE FISH
**1½ lb assorted fish fillets such as angler
fish, trout, sea bream, cod**
⅔ cup low-fat, plain yogurt
½ to 1 Tbsp curry powder, or to taste
1 tsp paprika
1 tsp chili powder
3 Tbsp lemon juice
1 Tbsp grated lemon zest

FOR THE RICE
1¼ cups basmati rice
1 tsp paprika
8 scallions, trimmed and chopped
2 Tbsp chopped fresh cilantro

TO GARNISH
Cilantro sprigs and lemon wedges

TO SERVE
**Warm pita bread and tossed
green salad**

Rinse the fish fillets and pat dry. Cut into bite-size pieces and place in a shallow
dish. Blend the yogurt with the curry powder, paprika, chili powder, and lemon
juice and zest, then pour over the fish. Cover lightly and leave in the refrigerator for
at least 30 minutes.

Cook the rice in lightly salted boiling water for 12 minutes or until done, drain,
and stir in the paprika, scallions, and cilantro. Keep warm.

Lightly spray or brush your grill pan with oil then place on a moderate heat until hot.
Drain the fish and thread alternate pieces onto the skewers. Cook in the grill pan
for 3 to 4 minutes on each side or until done. Garnish and serve on top of the rice,
with warm strips of pita bread, and a tossed green salad.

Seared Scallop and Shrimp Tortillas

SEARED SCALLOP AND
SHRIMP TORTILLAS

THESE TORTILLAS MAKE AN IDEAL DINNER PARTY APPETIZER.

Serves **4**

Preparation time **12 to 15 minutes plus 30 minutes marinating time**

Cooking time **3 to 4 minutes**

12 fresh medium scallops, deveined

12 raw jumbo shrimp, heads removed, deveined, and peeled

2 Tbsp white wine vinegar

4 Tbsp olive oil

1 Tbsp liquid honey, warmed

1 to 1½ tsp crushed dried chillies

1½ cups sliced chestnut mushrooms

2 Tbsp chopped fresh cilantro

8 large flour tortillas

FOR THE CHILI MAYONNAISE

2 medium egg yolks *(see page 4)*

1 tsp Dijon mustard

1 Tbsp lemon juice

1¼ cups olive oil

½ to 1 tsp hot chili sauce, or to taste

Salt and freshly ground pepper

TO SERVE

Shredded lettuce and scallions, trimmed and cut into strips

TO GARNISH

Lemon wedges and paprika

Slice the scallops in half and place in a shallow dish with the shrimp. Blend the vinegar, oil, honey, and chillies together and pour over the shellfish. Cover and leave to marinate in the refrigerator for at least 30 minutes, occasionally spooning over the marinade.

Make the mayonnaise by beating the egg yolks with the mustard and lemon juice. Slowly beat in the oil until a thick consistency is reached. Add the hot chili sauce with seasoning to taste and set aside.

Lightly brush or spray your grill pan with oil then place on a moderate heat until hot. Drain the shellfish, reserving 2 tablespoons of the marinade, and add the mushrooms to the pan with the marinade. Cook for 1 minute, stirring occasionally. Add the shellfish to the pan and cook for 2 to 3 minutes or until the shrimp and scallops are just done. Sprinkle with cilantro.

Heat the tortillas as directed on the package. To serve, smear each tortilla with a little mayonnaise and add shredded lettuce and scallions. Top with the shellfish and mushroom mixture, roll up, dust with paprika, garnish with lemon wedges, and serve.

MACKEREL WITH BACON
AND PINE NUTS

FISH AND BACON MAKE A VERY GOOD COMBINATION, TRY IT FOR YOURSELF.

Rinse the mackerel, pat dry, and set aside. Heat the oil in a small pan and gently sauté the scallions for 2 minutes. Remove from the heat and stir in the orange zest, pine nuts, raisins, apricots, bread crumbs, and seasoning to taste. Mix to a stiff consistency with the egg and use to stuff the cavities of the fish.

Place the bacon on a chopping board and using a round-bladed knife, stretch the bacon slightly and wrap two slices round each fish, securing with a toothpick.

Lightly brush or spray your grill pan with oil then place on a moderate heat until hot. Cook the fish over a moderate heat for 5 to 6 minutes each side, remove from the pan, and discard the toothpicks.

Garnish and serve with the potatoes and spinach or salad.

Serves **4**
Preparation time **12 minutes**
Cooking time **12 to 14 minutes**

4 small whole 8-oz mackerel (or use other fish such as red mullet or trout), cleaned
1 Tbsp oil
4 scallions, trimmed and chopped
1 Tbsp grated orange zest
2 Tbsp toasted pine nuts
½ cup raisins
½ cup dried apricots, chopped
1 cup fresh bread crumbs
Salt and freshly ground black pepper
1 medium egg, beaten
8 Canadian bacon slices

TO GARNISH
Orange zest and herbs

TO SERVE
Sautéed potatoes and wilted spinach or salad

LOBSTER TAILS WITH
LEMON AND TARRAGON MAYONNAISE

LOBSTER IS REGARDED BY MANY AS THE MOST PRIZED OF ALL SHELLFISH. THIS IS A SIMPLE
BUT ELEGANT WAY TO SERVE IT.

Beat the egg yolks with the mustard, lemon juice, and zest then pour into a blender and process for 30 seconds. With the motor still running, slowly pour in the oil in a thin stream, ensuring that the oil is incorporated before adding more. When all the oil has been added, scrape into a small bowl and stir in the tarragon with seasoning to taste. If the mayonnaise is too thick, add a little more lemon juice.

Place the lobster tails on a chopping board with the underside uppermost. With a large sharp knife slit down the center to straighten and to prevent the tails curling during cooking.

Lightly brush or spray your grill pan with oil then place on a moderate heat until hot. Add the tablespoon of oil then add the lobster tails, slit-side down. Cook for 5 minutes then add the lemon juice and continue to cook for 3 to 5 minutes or until done and the shells have turned pink. Remove from the pan and set aside.

Add the butter to the pan and heat until melted. Carefully swirl the juices together then pour over the lobster tails.

Garnish and serve with the potatoes.

Serves **4**
Preparation time **10 minutes**
Cooking time **8 to 10 minutes**

FOR THE MAYONNAISE

2 medium egg yolks *(see page 4)*
1 tsp Dijon mustard
3 Tbsp lemon juice
1 Tbsp fine grated lemon zest
1¼ cups olive oil
2 Tbsp chopped fresh tarragon
Salt and freshly ground pepper

FOR THE LOBSTER

4 fresh lobster tails
1 Tbsp olive oil
4 Tbsp lemon juice
½ stick sweet butter

TO GARNISH

Salad leaves and cherry tomatoes

TO SERVE

New potatoes

GRILLED TUNA WITH MANGO SALSA

THIS DELICIOUS FRUITY SALSA GOES WELL WITH MANY OF THE OTHER DISHES IN THIS BOOK. TRY IT WITH
CHICKEN, TURKEY, OR PORK TO PROVIDE AN ALTERNATIVE ACCOMPANIMENT.

Combine all the ingredients for the Salsa in a bowl, cover, and refrigerate for at least 30 minutes to allow the flavors to develop.

Lightly rinse the tuna, pat dry, and place in a shallow dish. Blend the coconut milk, paprika, chillies, lemon grass, and fruit juice and pour over the tuna. Cover and leave in the refrigerator for at least 30 minutes, spooning the marinade occasionally over the fish.

Cook the sweet potato slices for about 5 minutes or until almost tender, drain, and reserve. Lightly spray or brush your grill pan with oil then pour in 1 tablespoon of the oil. Place on a moderate heat until hot. Add half the potato slices and cook, turning once, until hot and slightly charred. Remove and keep warm. Repeat with the remaining oil and potato slices.

Drain the fish and cook in the pan for 3 to 4 minutes on each side or until tender.

Serve the tuna on top of the potato slices with the Mango Salsa and salad leaves.

Serves **4**
Preparation time **10 to 12 minutes
plus 30 minutes marinating time**
Cooking time **15 minutes for
the potatoes, 6 to 8 minutes
for the fish**

FOR THE MANGO SALSA

**1 small, ripe mango, peeled, pitted,
and diced fine**
4 scallions, trimmed and sliced fine
**1 small jalapeño chili, seeded and
chopped fine**
**2 ripe tomatoes, seeded and
chopped**
2 tsp liquid honey, warmed
2 Tbsp chopped fresh cilantro

FOR THE FISH

Four 5-oz fresh tuna steaks
⅔ cup coconut milk
1 tsp paprika
**2 green serrano chillies, seeded
and sliced**
**2 stalks lemon grass, outer leaves
removed and chopped**
¼ cup mango or orange juice
**1½ lb sweet potatoes, peeled and
cut into thick slices**
1 to 2 Tbsp oil

TO SERVE

**Bitter salad leaves such as frisée,
radicchio, and arugula**

ORIENTAL SEA BASS

THIS RECIPE WILL WORK WELL WITH ANY FISH FILLETS, BUT MAKE
SURE THAT YOU REMOVE THE LITTLE PIN BONES FROM THE FILLETS
BEFORE MARINATING.

Serves **4**
Preparation time **4 minutes plus**
  30 minutes marinating time
Cooking time **6 to 8 minutes**

4 small sea bass, filleted
2 Tbsp dark soy sauce
4 Tbsp medium-dry sherry
2 Tbsp lemon juice
4 garlic cloves, peeled and crushed
1 jalapeño chili, seeded and sliced
1 Tbsp liquid honey, warmed

TO GARNISH
Chopped fresh cilantro

TO SERVE
Oriental Salad *(see page 102)* **and**
  freshly cooked white and wild rice

Lightly rinse and dry the fish fillets and place in a shallow dish. Blend the soy
sauce, sherry, lemon juice, garlic, and chili with the honey and pour over the fillets.
Cover lightly and leave in refrigerator for at least 30 minutes. Spoon the marinade
occasionally over the fish.

Lightly spray or brush your grill pan with oil then place on a moderate heat
until hot. Drain the fillets, reserving 2 tablespoons of the marinade, and cook
in the pan for 3 to 4 minutes on each side or until tender. Spoon over a little
marinade at the end of the cooking time. Remove from the pan and place on
warm serving plates.

Sprinkle with the chopped cilantro and serve with the salad and rice.

Charred Cod with Pesto

CHARRED COD WITH PESTO

TRY A MINT PESTO WITH THIS DISH: FOR A CHANGE SUBSTITUTE
THE BASIL LEAVES WITH FRESH MINT LEAVES AND USE TOASTED
HAZELNUTS INSTEAD OF THE PINE NUTS.

Serves **4**
Preparation time **5 minutes plus**
  30 minutes marinating time
Cooking time **6 to 10 minutes**

FOR THE PESTO
1 cup fresh basil leaves
2 Tbsp toasted pine nuts
3 to 4 garlic cloves, peeled and chopped
1 Tbsp lemon juice
½ cup olive oil
2 Tbsp grated fresh Parmesan cheese

FOR THE FISH
Four 5-oz cod fillets or steaks
2 Tbsp olive oil
4 Tbsp lemon juice
3 garlic cloves, peeled and sliced
1 Tbsp roughly torn basil leaves

TO SERVE
Freshly cooked pasta noodles, tossed in
  2 Tbsp melted butter, 1 Tbsp grated
  lemon zest, and a little chopped basil;
  sliced tomatoes; sliced black olives

TO GARNISH
Basil leaves

Place the basil leaves with the pine nuts, garlic, and lemon juice in a food processor
and blend for 30 seconds. Keeping the motor running, slowly add the olive oil and
then stir in the Parmesan cheese. Scrape into a small bowl, cover, and set aside.

Lightly rinse the fish, pat dry, and place in a shallow dish. Blend the olive oil and
lemon juice with the garlic and torn basil leaves and pour over the fish. Cover lightly
and leave in the refrigerator for at least 30 minutes.

Lightly spray or brush your grill pan with oil then place on a moderate heat until hot.
Drain the fish and cook in the pan for 3 to 5 minutes on each side, depending on
thickness, until done.

Remove from the pan and spoon over a little of the pesto and serve with the freshly
cooked noodles, sliced tomatoes, and black olives. Garnish with basil leaves and
serve the remaining pesto separately.

BLISTERED SHRIMP WITH
RED BELL PEPPER SAUCE

THESE MAKE AN IDEAL DINNER PARTY APPETIZER OR SERVE WITH DRINKS, USING THE SAUCE AS A DIP.
YOU WILL NEED 8 TO 16 SMALL WOODEN SKEWERS OR TOOTHPICKS.

Peel the shrimp, removing the black vein down the backbone, and place in a shallow dish. Blend the oil, vinegar, chillies, and garlic and pour over the shrimp. Cover lightly and leave to marinate in the refrigerator for at least 30 minutes, spooning the marinade over the shrimp a few times.

Cut the green and yellow bell peppers into bite-size pieces and set aside.

Heat the oil in a small pan and sauté the shallots for 3 minutes. Add the chopped red bell peppers and add to the pan with the broth and tomato juice. Bring to a boil then simmer for 12 minutes or until soft. Remove from the heat, cool slightly, then pass through a processor or blender to form a purée. Add the balsamic vinegar. If liked rub through a fine sieve to achieve a smooth consistency. Set aside.

Drain the shrimp, reserving the marinade. Cut each bacon slice into three shorter strips and wrap round the shrimp. Thread the shrimp with the bell peppers onto the skewers, brushing the bell peppers with the marinade.

Lightly brush or spray your grill pan with oil then place on a moderate heat until hot. Add 1 tablespoon of the marinade then cook the prawns for 2 to 4 minutes each side or until the shrimp have turned pink and the peppers are charred.

Garnish with the parsley and salad then serve with the Pepper Sauce and bread.

Serves **8 as an appetizer, 4 as a main meal**
Preparation time **12 minutes plus 30 minutes marinating time**
Cooking time **19 to 23 minutes**

10 oz raw jumbo shrimp, heads removed if preferred
3 Tbsp olive oil
2 Tbsp balsamic vinegar
1 to 2 Tbsp dried crushed chillies
2 garlic cloves, peeled and crushed
1 small green and 1 small yellow bell pepper, seeded
10 to 12 bacon slices

FOR THE RED BELL PEPPER SAUCE
1 Tbsp oil
2 shallots, peeled and chopped
3 red bell peppers, skinned, seeded, and chopped
1¼ cups broth
⅔ cup tomato juice
1 Tbsp balsamic vinegar

TO GARNISH
Parsley sprigs and salad

TO SERVE
Warm crusty French bread

STUFFED RED MULLET

GRAPE LEAVES ARE USUALLY PRESERVED IN BRINE SO IT IS IMPORTANT TO SOAK THEM THOROUGHLY BEFORE USE.

Cover the grape leaves with boiling water and leave for 20 minutes, drain, and rinse thoroughly in cold water. Pat dry and set aside.

Rinse the fish, pat dry on paper towels, and set aside.

Heat 2 teaspoons of oil in a pan and sauté the scallions for 2 minutes. Remove from the heat and stir in the apricots, hazelnuts, orange zest, dill, bread crumbs, and seasoning. Mix with the egg yolk and sufficient orange juice to make a stiff consistency. Use to stuff the cavities of the fish. Wrap each fish in the grape leaves, encasing them completely, and secure with either twine or toothpicks.

Lightly brush or spray your grill pan with oil then place on a moderate heat until hot. Add the remaining oil and then place the fish in the pan and cook for 4 minutes each side or until done and the grape leaves are charred.

Remove the twine or toothpicks, garnish, and serve with the Saffron-flavored Couscous and greens.

Serves **4**
Preparation time **12 minutes**
Cooking time **10 minutes**

12 to 16 grape leaves, depending
   on size
4 small red mullet or other small
   whole fish, cleaned and
   descaled
2 Tbsp oil
4 scallions, trimmed and chopped
½ cup dried apricots, chopped
   fine
2 Tbsp chopped hazelnuts
1 Tbsp grated orange zest
1 Tbsp chopped fresh dill
½ cup fresh bread crumbs
Salt and freshly ground black
   pepper
1 medium egg yolk
2 to 3 Tbsp orange juice

TO GARNISH
Orange wedges and dill sprigs

TO SERVE
Saffron-flavored Couscous
   (see page 64) and stir-fried
   spring greens

GRILLED SARDINES WITH
GINGER AND MINT BUTTER

FRESH HERBS ARE WIDELY AVAILABLE BUT IF YOU ARE FORTUNATE
ENOUGH TO HAVE YOUR OWN HERB GARDEN THIS IS A BLESSING AS
THE FLAVOR OF FRESHLY PICKED HERBS IS SECOND TO NONE.

Serves **2 to 4**
Preparation time **10 minutes plus
   2 hours marinating time**
Cooking time **8 to 12 minutes**

8 small sardines, cleaned
2 Tbsp grated fresh ginger
2 Tbsp chopped fresh mint
**1 jalapeño chili, seeded and chopped
   fine**
3 Tbsp lemon juice
4 Tbsp oil

FOR THE MINT BUTTER
¾ stick sweet butter, softened
1 Tbsp fine grated fresh ginger
2 Tbsp chopped fresh mint
1 Tbsp grated lemon zest
1 to 2 Tbsp lemon juice

TO GARNISH
Lemon wedges

TO SERVE
**Grilled bread (Toast the bread on
   the grill pan when the fish is nearly
   done) and endive, watercress, and
   orange salad**

Lightly rinse the fish and place in a shallow dish. Blend the ginger, mint, chili, lemon
juice, and oil and pour over the fish. Cover lightly and leave to marinate for at least 2
hours in the refrigerator.

Meanwhile blend all the ingredients for the butter, shape into a roll, wrap in waxed
paper, and chill for 30 minutes.

Lightly brush or spray your grill pan with oil then place on a moderate heat until
hot. Remove the fish from the marinade and cook, two to four fish at a time
(depending on the size of the pan and the fish) in the heated grill pan for 2 to 3
minutes each side.

When all the fish are done, top with a small piece of the flavored butter. Garnish with
lemon wedges and serve with toasted bread and the salad.

Chinese-style Swordfish

CHINESE-STYLE SWORDFISH

IF YOU CANNOT FIND DRIED CRUSHED CHILLIES, USE EITHER A WHOLE DRIED CHILI, CRUSHED, OR USE A FRESH CHILI BUT DOUBLE THE AMOUNT.

Serves **4**
Preparation time **10 to 12 minutes plus 30 minutes marinating time**
Cooking time **6 to 8 minutes**

FOR THE DIPPING SAUCE

3 Tbsp light soy sauce
½ to 1 tsp crushed dried chillies
1 tsp light soft brown sugar
2 Tbsp orange juice

FOR THE FISH

Four 5-oz swordfish steaks
2 red serrano chillies, seeded and chopped

3 garlic cloves, peeled and crushed
2 Tbsp grated fresh ginger
1 Tbsp light soft brown sugar
3 Tbsp black bean sauce
1 Tbsp grated lime zest
3 Tbsp lime juice
2 Tbsp soy sauce
4 Tbsp sake or dry sherry

TO GARNISH

1 Tbsp chopped fresh cilantro

TO SERVE

Freshly cooked egg noodles and Oriental Salad *(see page 102)*

Blend the ingredients for the sauce and leave to allow the flavors to develop.

Wipe the fish steaks and place in a shallow dish. Blend the chillies, garlic, ginger, and sugar with the black bean sauce, lime zest and juice, the soy sauce, and sake or dry sherry. Pour over the steaks and leave in the refrigerator for 30 minutes to allow the flavors to develop.

When ready to cook, lightly brush or spray your grill pan with oil then place on a moderate heat until hot. Drain the the swordfish steaks, place in the pan, and cook for 3 to 4 minutes on each side until done. Remove from the pan and sprinkle immediately with the chopped cilantro.

Serve with the dipping sauce, the noodles, and salad.

TILAPIA IN BANANA LEAVES

WHEN USING BANANA LEAVES IT IS IMPORTANT TO SOFTEN THEM FIRST. PLACE IN A BOWL AND POUR OVER BOILING WATER, LEAVE FOR A FEW MINUTES, THEN DRAIN AND USE AS DIRECTED. MAKE THE FLAVORED BUTTER BY BEATING TWO TEASPOONS OF WASABI PASTE INTO 1 STICK SOFTENED BUTTER WITH 1 TO 2 TABLESPOONS OF LIME JUICE.

Wipe the fish fillets and set aside. Place all the ingredients except the banana leaves and lime slices in a food processor and blend to form a paste. Spread over the fish fillets.

Place the softened banana leaves on a clean surface and place the fillets in the center. Top with the prepared paste and lime slices. Fold the leaves over to encase the fish completely and secure with either fine twine or toothpicks.

Lightly brush or spray your grill pan with oil then place on a gentle heat. Add the fish and cook for 6 to 8 minutes each side or until the leaves turn brown and the fish is done.

Discard the twine or toothpicks and serve in the leaves so that the aroma is released when the parcels are opened.

Serve with lime quarters to squeeze over, the wasabi butter, steamed rice, and stir-fried vegetables.

Serves **4**
Preparation time **5 to 7 minutes**
Cooking time **12 to 16 minutes**

Four 8-oz tilapia or red snapper fillets
2 stalks lemon grass, outer leaves removed and chopped
2 garlic cloves, peeled and crushed
3 green serrano chillies, seeded and chopped
2 Tbsp grated fresh ginger
6 scallions, trimmed and chopped
1 tsp ground coriander
2 Tbsp lime juice
4 banana leaves, softened
2 limes, sliced

TO SERVE
Lime quarters, wasabi butter, steamed rice, and stir-fried vegetables

SALMON AND SHRIMP FISHCAKES

IF SWEET POTATOES ARE UNAVAILABLE, USE ORDINARY POTATOES, BUT INCREASE THE COOKING TIME SLIGHTLY.

Cut the potatoes into cubes and cook in lightly salted boiling water for 15 minutes or until tender. Drain, mash, and set aside.

Place the salmon and shrimp in a food processor and blend to form a rough purée. Transfer to a bowl and mix in the mashed potatoes.

Lightly rinse the zucchini and coarsely grate, then add to the fish with the lemon zest, cilantro, egg yolk, and seasoning to taste. Mix lightly then form into small cakes with dampened hands.

Coat in the flour and chill for 30 minutes.

Lightly brush or spray your grill pan with oil then place on a moderate heat until hot. Add 1 tablespoon of the oil and cook the fish cakes for 3 to 4 minutes each side, adding the extra oil halfway through cooking if required.

Garnish and serve with Hollandaise sauce, bread, and green salad.

Serves **4**
Preparation time **15 minutes**
   plus 30 minutes chilling time
Cooking time **21 to 23 minutes**

8 oz sweet potatoes, peeled
12 oz fresh salmon fillets, skinned
6 oz raw fresh jumbo shrimp, shelled
1 small zucchini (about 4 oz in weight), trimmed
Grated zest of 1 lemon
2 to 3 Tbsp chopped fresh cilantro
1 medium egg yolk
Salt and freshly ground black pepper
1 to 2 Tbsp white all-purpose flour
1 to 2 Tbsp sunflower oil

TO GARNISH
Lemon wedges and cilantro

TO SERVE
Hollandaise sauce, warm chunks of herb bread, and tossed green salad

BLISTERED NIÇOISE

A VARIATION ON THE EVER-POPULAR SALADE NIÇOISE, THIS VERSION USES BOTH FRESH TUNA AND SQUID AND SHOULD BE SERVED WARM.

Lightly rinse the tuna steaks and squid and pat dry. Cut the squid in half and make a criss-cross pattern over them, place with the tuna in a shallow dish. Blend the olive oil, lemon juice, garlic, and balsamic vinegar and pour over the fish. Cover lightly and leave in the refrigerator for at least 30 minutes. Spoon the marinade over the fish a few times.

Meanwhile cook the potatoes in lightly salted boiling water for 12 to 15 minutes or until tender when pierced with a fork. Drain and set aside.

Place the eggs in a small pan, cover with cold water, and bring to a boil. Simmer for 8 minutes, drain, and plunge into cold water. Shell when ready to use.

Rinse the beans and cook in lightly salted boiling water for 5 minutes or until tender, drain, plunge into cold water to refresh, drain again, and set aside.

Tear the lettuce into pieces and place in a salad bowl. Scatter over the tomatoes and yellow bell pepper.

Cut the artichoke hearts in half and arrange over the tomatoes with the potatoes and beans. Scatter with the olives. Cover and set aside.

Lightly spray or brush your grill pan with oil then place on a moderate heat until hot. Drain the tuna and squid. Cook the squid in the grill pan for 1 to 2 minutes on each side, pressing them down lightly in the pan to prevent them curling up, or until done. Remove from the pan. Cook the tuna in the grill pan for 2 to 3 minutes each side or until cooked then remove from the pan.

Flake the tuna into pieces and place with the squid on top of the salad.

Pour the remaining marinade into the pan, bring to a boil, and boil for 1 minute then pour over the tuna and squid, tossing lightly.

Shell the eggs and arrange on top of the salad, sprinkle with the parsley, and serve with crusty bread.

Serves **4 to 6**
Preparation time
  15 to 18 minutes plus 30 minutes marinating time
Cooking time **30 to 33 minutes**

FOR THE TUNA

Two 5-oz fresh tuna steaks

8 oz fresh baby squid, cleaned

2 Tbsp olive oil

3 Tbsp lemon juice

4 garlic cloves, peeled and crushed

2 Tbsp balsamic vinegar

FOR THE SALAD

8 oz baby new potatoes, scrubbed

3 medium eggs

10 oz green beans, trimmed

2 small heads Romaine lettuce, rinsed

8 to 10 cherry tomatoes, halved

1 yellow bell pepper, seeded and sliced thin

1¼ cups canned or bottled artichoke hearts, drained

¼ cup black olives, pitted

TO GARNISH

2 Tbsp chopped flat-leaf parsley

TO SERVE

Crusty bread

BEEF

CIABATTA STEAK SANDWICH

THIS SANDWICH MAKES A DELICIOUS LUNCH OR LIGHT SUPPER. TRY VARYING THE BREAD, ACCORDING TO PERSONAL PREFERENCE.

Lightly brush or spray your grill pan with oil then place on a moderate heat until hot. Add 1 tablespoon of the oil then add the onions and garlic and cook for 3 minutes or until done but still crisp. Remove from the pan and keep warm. Add the remaining oil to the pan.

Season the steak with the salt and pepper then cook in the pan for 1 to 2 minutes each side or until sealed. Add the balsamic vinegar and continue to cook the steaks for 2 to 4 minutes or until done to personal preference.

Meanwhile cut the loaf into four and split in half horizontally. Lightly toast in the grill pan (or under the broiler) then arrange the salad leaves on the base of the bread, top with the steak, the grated cheese, and the onions. Sprinkle with the parsley. Place the top slice of bread in position and serve immediately with mustard or horseradish sauce on the side.

Serves **4**
Preparation time **5 minutes**
Cooking time **7 to 10 minutes**

2 Tbsp sunflower oil
2 large red onions, peeled and
    sliced
2 to 3 garlic cloves, peeled and
    sliced
Four 4-oz pieces fillet steak
Freshly milled rock salt and
    freshly ground black pepper
1 Tbsp balsamic vinegar
1 large ciabatta loaf
Gruyère cheese, sliced thin

TO SERVE
Arugula and radicchio leaves,
    2 Tbsp chopped flat-leaf parsley,
    mustard or horseradish sauce

BALSAMIC FILLET STEAKS

MAKE THE FLAVORED BUTTER AHEAD OF TIME, WRAP IN WAXED PAPER,
AND CHILL IN THE REFRIGERATOR UNTIL REQUIRED.

Wipe the steaks and place in a shallow dish. Scatter over the shallots. Blend the red wine, vinegar, oil, and sugar together and pour over the steaks, cover lightly, and leave to marinate in the refrigerator for at least 30 minutes.

Meanwhile cream the butter with the shallot, capers, parsley, and pepper, form into a roll, and wrap in waxed paper and refrigerate until required.

Cut the potatoes into ½-inch slices then cook in lightly salted boiling water for 5 minutes. Drain and set aside.

Lightly brush or spray your grill pan with oil then place on a moderate heat until hot and almost smoking. Drain the steaks, reserving the marinade, and cook for 1½ to 3 minutes or until done to personal preference. Remove from the pan and keep warm.

Reheat the pan, add 1 tablespoon of the oil, and cook half the blanched potato slices for 2 to 3 minutes until golden and lightly charred, remove, drain on paper towels, and keep warm. Cook the remaining potatoes in a further tablespoon of the oil. Keep warm.

Meanwhile strain the marinade then boil vigorously for 8 to 10 minutes or until reduced by about half.

Add the remaining oil to the pan and quickly grill the asparagus spears for 2 to 3 minutes or until lightly charred.

Arrange the potato slices on warmed serving plates, top with the steaks, a piece of the flavored butter, pour a little of the sauce around, and serve with the asparagus spears.

Serves **4**
Preparation time **12 minutes plus
30 minutes marinating time**
Cooking time **21 to 27 minutes**

Four 4-oz fillet steaks
2 shallots, peeled and sliced
1¼ cups red wine
2 Tbsp balsamic vinegar
1 Tbsp olive oil
2 tsp light soft brown sugar

FOR THE BUTTER

¾ stick sweet butter, softened
**1 shallot, peeled and chopped or
grated very fine**
1 Tbsp capers, drained and chopped
2 Tbsp chopped fresh parsley
Freshly ground black pepper

TO SERVE

**1½ lb large potatoes, scrubbed or
peeled**
3 to 4 Tbsp olive oil
**6 oz asparagus spears, trimmed
and cut in half if large**

DEVILED STEAKS

FOR A HOTTER FLAVOR, TRY ADDING A LITTLE HOT CHILI SAUCE
TO THE MARINADE.

Serves **4**
Preparation time **5 minutes plus
  30 minutes marinating time**
Cooking time **6 to 10 minutes**

Four 5-oz sirloin steaks
3 garlic cloves, peeled and crushed
2 Tbsp tomato paste
1 Tbsp Worcestershire sauce
1 tsp English mustard
2 to 3 tsp horseradish sauce
1 Tbsp balsamic vinegar
3 Tbsp lemon juice
3 Tbsp sunflower oil

TO SERVE
**4 medium ripe tomatoes, rinsed and cut
  in half**
**New potatoes and Provençal Green
  Beans (Cooked beans mixed with
  cooked onion, chopped tomatoes,
  and red bell pepper)**

TO GARNISH
Bay leaves and lemon wedges

Trim the steak, discarding any excess fat, wipe, and place in a shallow dish.
Blend the garlic with the tomato paste, Worcestershire sauce, mustard, horseradish
sauce, vinegar, lemon juice, and oil. Pour over the steaks, cover lightly, and leave
to marinate in the refrigerator for at least 30 minutes, spooning the marinade
occasionally over the steaks.

Lightly brush or spray your grill pan with oil then place on a moderate heat until hot.

Drain the steaks and cook in the pan for 2 to 4 minutes each side or until done
according to personal preference.

Add the halved tomatoes to the pan, cut-side down, and cook for 1 minute, turn and
cook for a further minute or until hot.

Serve the steaks with the tomatoes, potatoes, and beans and garnish with the bay
leaves and lemon wedges.

Skewered Spiced Beef

SKEWERED SPICED BEEF

WHEN MOLDING THE BEEF, PRESS AROUND THE SKEWERS FIRMLY WITH DAMPENED HANDS TO ENSURE THAT THE MEAT STAYS ON THE SKEWERS DURING COOKING.

Serves **4**
Preparation time **10 to 12 minutes**
Cooking time **8 to 10 minutes**

1 lb ground beef
4 garlic cloves, peeled and crushed
1 to 2 red jalapeño chillies, seeded and
   chopped fine
1 Tbsp grated lemon zest
1 to 1½ tsp ground ginger
1 tsp ground cinnamon
2 Tbsp chopped fresh cilantro

TO GARNISH
Chopped fresh cilantro

TO SERVE
**Warm pita bread, shredded lettuce, thinly
   sliced onions, thinly sliced seeded red
   bell pepper, and Yogurt and Cucumber
   Dip** *(see page 17)*

Place the ground beef in a bowl and add the garlic, chillies, lemon zest, spices, and chopped cilantro. Mix together until the mixture forms a ball then divide into eight and mold round eight small wooden skewers, leaving a space of at least 1 inch at one end.

Lightly brush or spray your grill pan with oil then place on a moderate heat until hot. Cook the beef skewers for 8 to 10 minutes, turning occasionally, or until done to personal preference.

Garnish and serve with warm pita bread, shredded lettuce, onions, red pepper, and the Yogurt and Cucumber Dip on the side.

PEPPERED STEAKS WITH
RED ONION MARMALADE

THE PIQUANCY OF THE MARMALADE WITH ITS HINT OF FIERY HEAT BEAUTIFULLY COMPLEMENTS THESE PEPPERED STEAKS.

Heat the oil and sauté the onion, garlic, and chili for 5 minutes. Add the sugar and vinegar and simmer gently for 5 minutes or until a thick consistency is formed. Stir in the raisins and heat for 2 minutes, then place in a small serving bowl and set aside.

Roughly crush the peppercorns and press over the steaks.

Lightly brush or spray your grill pan with oil then place on a moderate heat until hot. Cook the steaks for 3 to 5 minutes each side or until done to personal preference. Remove from the pan and keep warm.

Add the soy sauce and brandy to the pan juices and carefully swirl the pan to mix. Add the cream, heat for 1 minute, then pour over the steaks. Garnish and serve with the prepared marmalade, potatoes, and salad.

Serves **4**
Preparation time **10 minutes**
Cooking time **18 to 22 minutes**

FOR THE MARMALADE
1 Tbsp sunflower oil
2 large red onions, peeled and chopped
3 garlic cloves, peeled and crushed
1 red jalapeño chili, seeded and chopped
1 Tbsp dark soft brown sugar
2 Tbsp red wine vinegar
2 Tbsp raisins

FOR THE STEAKS
2 Tbsp mixed peppercorns
Four 5-oz sirloin steaks
2 Tbsp light soy sauce
2 Tbsp brandy
⅔ cup sour cream

TO GARNISH
Flat-leaf parsley

TO SERVE
Sautéed potatoes and tossed green salad

GARLIC STEAK FAJITAS WITH
RED ONION SALSA

THESE FAJITAS ARE EASY AND QUICK TO PREPARE, AN IDEAL STANDBY FOR UNEXPECTED GUESTS.

Wipe the steaks and, using a sharp knife, make small slits in each and insert the garlic slivers. Leave in the refrigerator for at least 30 minutes.

Combine all the ingredients for the Salsa then place in a bowl, cover, and leave in the refrigerator for 30 minutes to allow the flavors to develop.

Lightly brush or spray your grill pan with oil and place on a moderate heat until hot then pour in the olive oil and add the steaks. Cook for 2 to 3 minutes each side or to personal preference. Remove from the pan, leave for a minute to settle, then cut into thin slices.

To serve, place shredded lettuce on a warmed tortilla, top with steak, salsa, and avocado, spoon over a little mustard-flavored sour cream, sprinkle with crushed chillies, and roll up.

Serves **4**
Preparation time **8 minutes plus 30 minutes marinating time**
Cooking time **4 to 6 minutes**

Four 4-oz sirloin steaks
4 garlic cloves, peeled and cut into thin slivers
1 Tbsp olive oil

FOR THE SALSA
1 medium red onion, peeled and chopped fine
1 green jalapeño chili, seeded and chopped fine
One 2-in piece cucumber, peeled, seeded, and chopped fine
3 medium ripe tomatoes, seeded and chopped fine
1 tsp light soft brown sugar
2 Tbsp chopped fresh cilantro

TO SERVE
8 wheat tortillas, warmed
Shredded lettuce; 1 ripe avocado, peeled, pitted, cut into slices, and tossed in 2 Tbsp lime juice; ½ cup sour cream mixed with ½ to 1 tsp English or Dijon mustard; crushed chillies

BEEF TOURNEDOS WITH SEARED BELL PEPPER AND TOMATO COULIS

SKINNING BELL PEPPERS IN A GRILL PAN IS VERY EASY. THE PAN MUST BE HOT BEFORE YOU PRESS THE PEPPERS, SKIN-SIDE DOWN, ONTO THE SURFACE OF THE PAN.

Trim the steaks, wipe, and place in a shallow dish. Blend the mustard, vinegar, honey, and soy sauce and spoon over the steaks, cover lightly, and leave in the refrigerator for 30 minutes. Turn the steaks once during this time.

Meanwhile lightly brush or spray your grill pan with oil then place on a moderate heat until hot. Add the bell pepper quarters and cook for 8 to 10 minutes or until the skins have charred and the bell peppers are soft. Remove and place in a plastic bag, leave until cool enough to handle, then skin and chop.

Heat the oil in a small pan and sauté the garlic and shallots for 5 minutes. Add the bell peppers and tomato juice and simmer gently for 10 minutes or until soft. Pass through a processor or blender to form a purée and, if liked, rub through a sieve to obtain a smooth sauce, adding 2 to 3 tablespoons of water if too thick. Season to taste and reheat gently.

Wipe the grill pan and heat again until hot. Drain the steaks and cook for 2 to 4 minutes each side or until done to personal preference. Remove from the pan and keep warm.

Add the halved cherry tomatoes to the pan and cook for 1 to 2 minutes or until softened.

Arrange the steaks on warmed serving plates with the tomatoes and pour the Bell Pepper Coulis around. Garnish and serve with the scallion-flavored mashed potatoes and green beans or baby vegetables.

Serves **4**
Preparation time
  12 to 15 minutes plus 30 minutes marinating time
Cooking time **28 to 35 minutes**

Four 4-oz fillet or sirloin steaks
2 tsp whole-grain mustard
1 Tbsp balsamic vinegar
1 tsp liquid honey, warmed
2 Tbsp light soy sauce
12 cherry tomatoes, cut in half

FOR THE BELL PEPPER COULIS
3 red bell peppers, seeded and cut into quarters
1 Tbsp sunflower oil
2 garlic cloves, peeled and crushed
2 shallots, peeled and chopped
1¼ cups tomato juice
Freshly milled sea salt and freshly ground black pepper

TO GARNISH
Flat-leaf parsley and black pepper, to taste

TO SERVE
Mashed potatoes flavored with chopped scallions, green beans or baby vegetables

ORANGE AND GREEN PEPPERCORN SHISH KEBAB

FRESH GREEN PEPPERCORNS, NORMALLY PRESERVED IN BRINE, SHOULD BE RINSED WELL BEFORE USE. IF THESE ARE UNAVAILABLE, USE EITHER PINK PEPPERCORNS MIXED WITH BLACK PEPPERCORNS OR MIXED PEPPERCORNS. GROUND RED AND BLACK PEPPERCORNS ALSO WORK WELL.

Trim the steak, wipe, and cut into bite-size pieces. Place in a shallow bowl. Blend the orange zest, garlic, oregano, and peppercorns with the orange juice and oil. Pour over the steaks, cover lightly, and leave to marinate in the refrigerator for at least 30 minutes, spooning the marinade occasionally over the steak.

When ready to cook, drain the steak, reserving the marinade. Cut the oranges into wedges. Thread the steak, orange wedges, and bay leaves onto eight small wooden skewers and brush the oranges with a little of the marinade.

Lightly brush or spray your grill pan with oil then place on a moderate heat until hot. Cook the kabobs for 2 to 3 minutes each side, or to personal preference, brushing occasionally with the marinade.

When done, arrange on serving plates and serve with mayonnaise flavored with herbs of your choice, salads, and bread.

Serves **4**
Preparation time **5 minutes plus 30 minutes marinating time**
Cooking time **4 to 6 minutes**

1 lb sirloin steak
1 Tbsp grated orange zest
4 garlic cloves, peeled and crushed
2 Tbsp chopped fresh oregano
2 Tbsp fresh green peppercorns, drained or 1 Tbsp mixed dried peppercorns, roughly crushed
4 Tbsp orange juice
2 Tbsp olive oil
2 small oranges
8 to 12 fresh bay leaves

TO SERVE

Herb mayonnaise; endive, watercress, and orange salad; chargrilled bell pepper salad; and warm crusty bread

BEEF ROULADE WITH
RED WINE SAUCE

THIS BEEF DISH IS AN ELEGANT CHOICE FOR A SPECIAL OCCASION.

Blanch the asparagus spears in lightly boiling water for 2 minutes, drain and refresh in cold water, and drain again.

Trim the steaks, place between two sheets of waxed paper, and pound to a ¼-inch thickness. Spread with the mustard then cover with the Parma ham, the asparagus spears, and red bell pepper strips. Roll up and secure with fine twine or toothpicks.

Lightly brush or spray your grill pan with oil then place on a moderate heat until hot.
Add the Roulades and cook for 10 to 12 minutes, turning frequently, or until done to personal preference. Remove from the pan, discard the twine or toothpicks, and keep warm.

Add the red wine and jelly or honey to the juices left in the pan and boil for 3 minutes or until reduced. Reduce the heat and stir in the vinegar and seasoning to taste. Simmer for 1 minute then stir in the sour cream.

Slice the Roulades and arrange on warm serving plates, pour a little sauce over them, garnish, and serve with the mustard-flavored mashed potatoes and grilled radicchio.
(To grill radicchio, cut one large head into wedges and cook in the grill pan for 1 to 2 minutes or until wilted.)

Serves **4**
Preparation time **15 to 20 minutes**
Cooking time **16 to 18 minutes**

**8 baby asparagus spears, trimmed
 and stalks shaved if slightly tough**
Four 4-oz sirloin steaks
1 to 2 tsp Dijon mustard
**4 to 8 slices Parma ham, depending
 on size**
**1 red bell pepper, seeded, skinned,
 and sliced thin**

FOR THE WINE SAUCE
1¼ cups red wine
1 tsp red currant jelly or liquid honey
1 Tbsp raspberry or balsamic vinegar
Salt and freshly ground black pepper
3 Tbsp sour cream

TO GARNISH
Flat-leaf parsley

TO SERVE
**Mustard-flavored mashed potatoes
 and grilled radicchio**

THE PERFECT HAMBURGER

HAMBURGERS ARE A CLASSIC ALL-TIME FAVORITE. TRY THIS WAY OF COOKING THEM FOR A REAL OUTDOOR FLAVOR.
FOR BEST RESULTS, USE TOP-QUALITY GROUND BEEF.

Serves **4**
Preparation time **5 minutes**
Cooking time **7 to 11 minutes**

1 lb ground beef
3 shallots, peeled and chopped fine
1 to 2 tsp horseradish sauce
2 Tbsp chopped fresh parsley
Freshly milled sea salt and freshly ground
 black pepper
4 hamburger buns

TO SERVE
Assorted salad leaves, charred red bell peppers,
 selection of mustards, mayonnaise, tomato chutney,
 relishes, ketchup, and thick fries

Place the ground beef, shallots, horseradish, parsley, and seasoning to taste in a bowl. Mix lightly together with slightly wet hands and form into four burgers.

Lightly brush or spray your grill pan with oil then place on a moderate heat until hot. Cook the burgers for 3 to 5 minutes each side or until done to personal preference. Remove and keep warm.

Split the buns in half and place cut-side down on the grill pan and cook for 1 minute or until lightly grilled.

Place the salad leaves on the base of the buns, top with the charred red bell peppers, hamburger, and your choice of toppings. Close the buns and serve with fries.

BARBECUED STEAK KABOBS

THE LONGER YOU LEAVE THE STEAK TO MARINATE THE STRONGER THE FLAVOR AND MORE TENDER THE MEAT. WHEN MARINATING, ALWAYS ENSURE THAT YOU EITHER TURN THE FOOD OCCASIONALLY OR SPOON THE MARINADE OVER SO THAT ALL THE FOOD PICKS UP THE FLAVOR OF THE MARINADE.

Serves **4**
Preparation time **6 minutes plus**
 30 minutes marinating time
Cooking time **2 to 4 minutes**

1 lb sirloin steak
2 Tbsp olive oil
1 Tbsp dark soft brown sugar
3 Tbsp red wine vinegar
1 Tbsp Worcestershire sauce
2 tsp English mustard
1 Tbsp grated lemon zest
2 Tbsp tomato ketchup

TO GARNISH
Sliced radishes, radicchio,
 and arugula

TO SERVE
Warm potato and apple salad and
 warm French bread

Trim the steaks, cut into long thin strips, and place in a shallow dish. Blend the oil with the sugar, vinegar, Worcestershire sauce, mustard, lemon zest, and ketchup and pour over the steak. Cover loosely and leave in the refrigerator for at least 30 minutes, turning the strips occasionally.

When ready to cook, drain the strips and thread onto eight small wooden skewers.

Lightly brush or spray your grill pan with oil then place on a moderate heat until hot. Cook the kabobs for 1 to 2 minutes each side or until done to personal preference.

Garnish and serve with a potato and apple salad and French bread.

TEXAS KABOBS

IF YOU CANNOT FIND CORN ON THE COB STILL WITH ITS OUTER LEAVES, BLANCH IN BOILING WATER FOR 10 MINUTES THEN DRAIN THOROUGHLY AND COOK IN THE GRILL PAN FOR 10 TO 15 MINUTES OR UNTIL TENDER.

Trim the steak, cut into bite-size cubes, and place in a shallow dish. Blend the chili sauce, spices, and oil then stir in the lager and six chopped scallions. Pour over the steak cubes, cover lightly, and leave to marinate in the refrigerator for 30 minutes, occasionally spooning over the marinade.

Prepare the corn by carefully pulling down the outer leaves, but leaving them still fixed at the base, then discard the silky threads. Pull the outer leaves up and secure loosely with fine twine.

Lightly brush or spray your grill pan with oil then place on a moderate heat until hot. Cook the corn cobs for 15 to 20 minutes or until tender, turning frequently. Remove from the pan and leave in a warm place.

Drain the steak and thread onto wooden skewers with the remaining scallions cut into three pieces. Add to the pan and cook, turning frequently, for 3 to 4 minutes each side or until done to personal preference.

Serve with the cooked corn cobs, baked potatoes topped with sour cream and scallions.

Serves **4**
Preparation time **8 minutes plus**
   30 minutes marinating time
Cooking time **15 to 20 minutes for the**
   corn, 6 to 8 minutes for the kabobs

1 lb sirloin steak
2 Tbsp chili sauce
1 tsp chili powder, or to taste
1 tsp ground cumin
1 tsp paprika
Cayenne pepper to taste
1 Tbsp sunflower oil
⅔ cup lager or light ale
10 scallions
4 ears corn on the cob

TO SERVE
Baked potatoes, sour cream, and
   chopped scallions

THAI BEEF KABOBS

REMEMBER WHEN USING FRESH CHILLIES THAT THE HEAT IS NOT ONLY IN THE SEEDS BUT ALSO IN THE MEMBRANE TO WHICH THEY ARE ATTACHED. DO NOT TOUCH ANY SENSITIVE PARTS OF THE BODY UNTIL YOU HAVE THOROUGHLY WASHED YOUR HANDS. TO BE SAFE, WEAR RUBBER GLOVES WHEN HANDLING CHILLIES.

Serves **4**
Preparation time **6 to 8 minutes plus
  30 minutes marinating time**
Cooking time **4 to 8 minutes**

FOR THE DIPPING SAUCE
3 Tbsp light soy sauce
1 Tbsp mirin or sherry
1 Thai chili, seeded and chopped fine
2 scallions, trimmed and chopped fine

FOR THE KABOBS
1 lb sirloin steak
1 Tbsp grated fresh ginger
**2 lemon grass stalks, outer leaves
  removed and chopped**
**1 to 2 Thai chillies, seeded if preferred
  and chopped**
3 garlic cloves, peeled and crushed
4 Tbsp lime juice
2 Tbsp sunflower oil
2 Tbsp chopped fresh cilantro

TO SERVE
**Steamed rice, prepared Thai peanut
  sauce, Oriental Salad *(see page 102)*,
  and cashew nuts**

Blend the ingredients for the dipping sauce together and leave to allow the flavors to develop.

Trim the steak, cut into long thin strips, and place in a shallow dish. Scatter with the ginger, chopped lemon grass, chillies, and garlic. Blend with the lime juice and oil and pour over the steaks. Cover loosely and leave in the refrigerator for 30 minutes.

When ready to cook, drain the steak strips and thread onto eight lemon grass stalks or wooden skewers.

Lightly brush or spray your grill pan with oil then place on a moderate heat until hot. Cook the kabobs for 2 to 4 minutes each side or until done to personal preference.

Sprinkle with the chopped cilantro and serve with dipping sauce, rice, Thai-style peanut sauce, salad, and cashew nuts.

Beef Teriyaki with Sizzled Vegetables

BEEF TERIYAKI WITH
SIZZLED VEGETABLES

I PREFER TO USE JAPANESE SOY SAUCE, WHICH IS A COMPLETELY
NATURAL PRODUCT WITH NO ADDITIVES ADDED AT ANY TIME DURING
ITS STEEPING OR BREWING PROCESS.

Serves **4**
Preparation time **10 minutes plus**
  30 minutes marinating time
Cooking time **6 to 7 minutes**

Four 5-oz fillet steaks
3 Tbsp light soy sauce
2 Tbsp mirin or sherry
1 Tbsp sunflower oil
1 tsp liquid honey, warmed
3 garlic cloves, peeled and crushed
1 Tbsp grated fresh ginger

FOR THE SIZZLED VEGETABLES
2 small carrots, peeled and cut into
  julienne strips
4 celery stalks, trimmed and cut into
  thin strips
2 small zucchini, trimmed and cut
  into thin strips
1 small red bell pepper and
  1 small yellow bell pepper, seeded
  and sliced fine

TO SERVE
Freshly cooked egg noodles

Trim the steaks and place in a shallow dish. Blend the soy sauce, mirin or sherry,
oil, honey, garlic, and ginger and pour over the steaks. Cover loosely and leave in
the refrigerator for 30 minutes, spooning the marinade over occasionally.

Lightly brush or spray your grill pan with oil then place on a moderate heat
until hot. Drain the steaks, reserving the marinade, and cook in the pan for 1½
to 2 minutes each side or until done to personal preference. Remove from the
pan and keep warm.

Add 1 tablespoon of the marinade to the grill pan, add the carrot and celery strips
and cook for 1 minute, then add the remaining vegetables and cook for
a further 2 minutes or until cooked but still crisp. If you prefer slightly softer
vegetables, cook a little longer. Place on warm serving plates.

Slice the steaks and place on top of the vegetables and serve with freshly
cooked noodles.

BEEF PAUPIETTES

THE STEAKS MUST BE AS THIN AS POSSIBLE BEFORE THEY ARE STUFFED AND ROLLED.

Place the steaks between two sheets of waxed paper and pound with a meat mallet until ¼ inch thick. Set aside.

Heat the oil in a small pan and sauté the shallots and mushrooms for 3 minutes. Remove from the heat and stir in the prunes, orange zest, bread crumbs, parsley, and seasoning to taste. Bind together with the egg then spread over the steaks. (Roll any remaining stuffing into small balls, coat in the flour, and refrigerate until required.) Roll up the steaks into small roulades and secure with fine twine or toothpicks.

Lightly brush or spray your grill pan with oil and place on a moderate heat until hot. Add the steaks and cook for 6 to 8 minutes or until done to personal preference. Remove from the pan, discard the twine or toothpicks and leave to settle for 2 minutes before slicing. Cook any stuffing balls in the pan, adding the oil if required.

Heat the wine, broth, and shallots. Simmer for 10 minutes. Add the jelly and seasoning to taste. Cream the butter and flour together then bring the wine mixture to a boil and whisk in small spoonfuls of the butter and flour paste. Cook, whisking until thickened.

On warmed serving plates, arrange the slices of steak on a bed of caramelized red and white onions. Serve with the sauce and freshly cooked vegetables.

Serves **4**
Preparation time **15 minutes**
Cooking time **30 to 32 minutes**

Four 5-oz sirloin steaks
1 Tbsp oil
2 shallots, peeled and chopped fine
1 cup field mushrooms, wiped and chopped
¾ cup ready-to-eat prunes, pitted and chopped fine
1 Tbsp grated orange zest
1 cup fresh white bread crumbs
1 Tbsp chopped fresh parsley
Salt and freshly ground black pepper
1 small egg, beaten
1 Tbsp white all-purpose flour
1 to 2 Tbsp sunflower oil

FOR THE SAUCE

1¼ cups red wine
¾ cup beef broth
2 shallots, peeled and chopped
1 tsp red wine jelly or red currant jelly
2 Tbsp butter
3 Tbsp all-purpose flour

TO SERVE

Caramelized red and white onions, new potatoes, freshly cooked baby carrots, French beans

LAMB

SKEWERED LAMB WITH
RED CURRANT COULIS

LAMB AND RED CURRANTS ARE A DELICIOUS COMBINATION OF FLAVORS. BECAUSE RED CURRANTS ARE ONLY IN SEASON FOR A SHORT TIME, IT IS WORTH FREEZING A GOOD SUPPLY, TO USE THROUGHOUT THE YEAR.

Place the cubed lamb in a shallow dish. Heat the red currant jelly with the vinegar, soy sauce, and oil and stir until blended. Pour over the lamb and stir well. Lightly cover and leave in the refrigerator for at least 30 minutes. Spoon the marinade occasionally over the lamb.

Shred the sprigs of rosemary of a few of the lower side sprigs and when ready to cook, drain the lamb and thread onto the rosemary sprigs. Alternatively, use wooden skewers.

Meanwhile make the coulis by gently cooking the red currants with the mint sprigs, sugar, and vinegar. Simmer for 10 minutes or until tender then pass through a fine sieve to form a smooth sauce. Set aside.

Lightly brush or spray your grill pan with oil then place on a moderate heat until hot. Cook the lamb for 3 to 5 minutes each side or until done to personal preference.

Garnish with extra fresh red currants and rosemary sprigs and serve with the coulis, new potatoes, and Chargrilled Mediterranean Vegetables.

Serves **4**
Preparation time **10 minutes**
  plus 30 minutes marinating time
Cooking time **16 to 20 minutes**

1 lb boneless lean lamb such as
  leg sirloin chops, cubed
2 Tbsp red currant jelly
3 Tbsp raspberry vinegar
2 tsp soy sauce
2 Tbsp sunflower oil
8 fresh rosemary sprigs

FOR THE COULIS
⅔ cup fresh red currants, removed
  from stalks and rinsed
2 to 3 sprigs mint
1 to 2 Tbsp soft brown sugar,
  or to taste
1 Tbsp raspberry vinegar

TO GARNISH
Red currants and a few
  rosemary sprigs

TO SERVE
New potatoes, tossed in chopped
  mint; and Chargrilled
  Mediterranean Vegetables
  (see page 106)

LAMB BROCHETTES WITH
MUSHROOM AND BASIL SAUCE

ROSÉ OR BLUSH WINE IS NOT OFTEN USED IN COOKING BUT CAN PRODUCE INTERESTING AND UNUSUAL RESULTS. HERE IT GIVES A BEAUTIFUL ROSÉ COLOR TO THE FINISHED SAUCE.

Place the mushrooms in a small bowl, cover with almost boiling water, and leave to soak for 30 minutes. Drain, reserving the liquor, and set aside.

Wipe the lamb and cut into bite-size pieces and place in a shallow dish. Blend the soaking liquor with the chopped basil, lemon zest and juice, and the oil and pour over the lamb. Cover loosely and leave in the refrigerator for 30 minutes spooning the marinade occasionally over the lamb.

Lightly brush or spray your grill pan with oil then place on a moderate heat until hot. Drain the lamb and thread alternately onto eight small wooden skewers with the bay leaves and zucchini pieces. Cook the brochettes in the pan for 8 to 10 minutes, with about 2 tablespoons of the marinade, turning occasionally, or until done.

Meanwhile place the wine in a small pan and boil vigorously for 5 to 8 minutes or until reduced by half. (If a thicker sauce is desired, blend 2 teaspoons of cornstarch with 1 tablespoon of water and stir into the reduced wine, then proceed as follows.) Add the red currant jelly, cream, and rehydrated mushrooms and simmer until the mushrooms are hot. Stir in the chopped basil.

Serve the brochettes sitting on a bed of rice and drizzle with the sauce.

Serves **4**
Preparation time
  5 minutes plus 30 minutes soaking time
  for the mushrooms and 30 minutes
  marinating time
Cooking time **13 to 18 minutes**

1 Tbsp dried porcini mushrooms
1 lb lean lamb such as fillet or leg
3 Tbsp chopped fresh basil
Grated zest and juice of 1 lemon
2 Tbsp olive oil
8 to 12 fresh bay leaves
2 small zucchini, trimmed and cut into
  bite-size pieces

FOR THE SAUCE
1 cup rosé (blush) wine
1 Tbsp red currant jelly
2 Tbsp heavy cream
2 Tbsp chopped fresh basil

TO SERVE
Freshly cooked rice, mixed with skinned,
  seeded, and chopped tomatoes,
  chopped basil, and grated lemon zest

SPICED LAMB BITES

THE SECRET OF THESE LITTLE MORSELS IS TO ENSURE THAT YOU MAKE THEM QUITE SMALL AND THAT YOU PRESS THE MIXTURE FIRMLY TOGETHER. TO SAVE TIME YOU COULD PUT ALL THE INGREDIENTS IN A FOOD PROCESSOR AND BLEND FOR A MINUTE OR TWO. THIS WILL GIVE THE MIXTURE A SMOOTHER TEXTURE.

Place the ground lamb in a mixing bowl with the remaining ingredients and mix together until the mixture forms a ball in the center of the bowl. Shape into small balls about the size of a small apricot.

Lightly brush or spray your grill pan with oil then place on a moderate heat until hot. Cook the bites for 8 to 10 minutes, turning frequently or until done to personal preference. Remove and drain on paper towels.

Warm the pita breads in the preheated grill pan for 1 minute then split to form pockets. Fill with shredded lettuce and cucumber and place the cooked bites on top. Spoon over a little yogurt and salsa. Garnish with chopped cilantro.

Serves **4**
Preparation time **10 minutes**
Cooking time **9 to 11 minutes**

1 lb ground lamb
1 tsp ground cumin
1 tsp ground coriander
2 large garlic cloves, peeled
   and crushed
1 to 2 red serrano chillies, seeded
   and chopped fine
1 Tbsp grated lemon zest
2 Tbsp chopped fresh cilantro

TO SERVE

4 to 8 pita breads, depending
   on size; shredded lettuce and
   cucumber; low-fat, plain yogurt;
   salsa

TO GARNISH

Chopped cilantro

CARAMELIZED LAMB
WITH VEGETABLES

THE CARROTS AND CELERY FOR THIS DISH MUST BE CUT VERY THIN SO THAT THEY ARE NOT
TOO CRISP AFTER COOKING.

Trim off any excess fat from the chops, wipe, then place in a shallow dish. Blend the sugar with the allspice, vinegar, oil, and port then pour over the chops, cover lightly, and leave in the refrigerator for at least 30 minutes. Turn the chops at least once during marinating.

Lightly brush or spray your grill pan with oil then place on a moderate heat until hot. Drain the chops and cook in the pan for 5 to 6 minutes on each side or until done to personal preference. Remove and keep warm.

Add the carrots and celery to the pan and cook, stirring for 3 minutes, add the zucchini and cashew nuts and continue to cook for 2 to 3 minutes or until done but still crunchy. Garnish the chops and serve with the sizzled vegetables and saffron-flavored couscous.

Serves **4**
Preparation time **12 minutes**
   plus 30 minutes marinating time
Cooking time **15 to 18 minutes**

4 large lamb shoulder arm chops
1 Tbsp dark soft brown sugar
2 tsp allspice
2 Tbsp white wine vinegar
2 Tbsp walnut or olive oil
3 Tbsp port

TO GARNISH

Deep-fried carrot and zucchini
  thin sticks

TO SERVE

8 oz carrots, peeled and cut into
  thin sticks
4 celery stalks, trimmed and cut
  into thin strips
1 zucchini trimmed and cut into
  sticks
2 Tbsp cashew nuts
Freshly cooked saffron couscous
  (see page 64)

LAMB STEAKS WITH
GARLIC AND ROSEMARY

THIS RECIPE IS VERY QUICK AND EASY TO PREPARE AND COOK. IF TIME IS REALLY SHORT YOU CAN SHORTEN THE MARINATING TIME BY HALF.

Wipe the steaks and, using a sharp knife, make small slits on both sides then insert the slivers of garlic and rosemary. Place in a shallow dish and sprinkle over the orange zest and shallots. Blend the oil and vinegar and pour over the steaks. Cover lightly and leave in the refrigerator for 30 minutes, turning the steaks occasionally.

Lightly brush or spray your grill pan with oil then place on a moderate heat until hot. Drain the steaks and cook in the pan for 4 to 6 minutes or until done to personal preference. Garnish with rosemary sprigs and orange zest and serve with the potatoes and ratatouille.

Serves **4**
Preparation time **5 minutes
plus 30 minutes marinating time**
Cooking time **4 to 6 minutes**

**Four 4-oz boneless lamb leg
sirloin steaks**
**3 garlic cloves, peeled and cut
into slivers**
**A few small fresh rosemary
sprigs**
1 Tbsp grated orange zest
**2 shallots, peeled and sliced into
wedges**
2 Tbsp olive oil
3 Tbsp red wine vinegar

TO GARNISH
Rosemary sprigs and orange zest

TO SERVE
**Diced sautéed potatoes with onion
and garlic, ratatouille**

LAMB WITH APRICOT RELISH

THE RELISH SERVED WITH THIS LAMB DISH WOULD WORK WELL WITH MANY OTHER DISHES. THINNED DOWN A LITTLE IT MAKES A GOOD SUBSTITUTE FOR GRAVY TO SERVE WITH ROAST LAMB.

Wipe the steaks and if thick make three diagonal slashes across each. Blend the garlic, shallots, mint, apricot or orange juice, and vinegar and pour over the steaks. Cover loosely and leave in the refrigerator for 30 minutes, turning at least once during this time.

Meanwhile make the relish. Place all the ingredients in a small pan and simmer gently for 10 minutes or until a thick consistency is formed. Set aside.

Lightly brush or spray your grill pan with oil then place on a moderate heat until hot. Add 1 tablespoon of the oil. Remove the lamb steaks from the marinade and cook in the pan for 5 to 6 minutes each side or until done to personal preference, adding the extra oil if necessary. Garnish and serve with the relish, the potatoes, and the spinach and bell pepper.

Serves **4**
Preparation time
  8 to 10 minutes plus 30 minutes marinating time
Cooking time **20 to 22 minutes**

Four 5-oz lamb leg steaks
4 garlic cloves, peeled and crushed
2 shallots, peeled and sliced
2 Tbsp chopped fresh mint
⅔ cup apricot or orange juice
2 Tbsp balsamic vinegar
1 to 2 Tbsp sunflower oil

FOR THE RELISH
1 cup dried apricots, chopped fine
1 Tbsp dark soft brown sugar
1 tsp ground cinnamon
6 Tbsp orange juice
1 Tbsp butter
1 Tbsp balsamic vinegar

TO GARNISH
Mint leaves

TO SERVE
Sautéed potatoes, wilted spinach mixed with chopped grilled yellow bell pepper

LAMB STEAKS WITH POLENTA
AND EGGPLANT PESTO

THE EGGPLANT PESTO MAKES A WELCOME CHANGE FROM THE TRADITIONAL BASIL PESTO
AND WORKS WELL WITH MANY DIFFERENT MEATS.

Trim the eggplant and slice thickly. Sprinkle with salt and leave for 30 minutes then rinse and thoroughly dry on paper towels.

Lightly brush or spray your grill pan with oil then place on a moderate heat until hot. Cook the eggplant slices for 1 minute on each side or until griddle marks have been formed. Add a further 2 to 3 tablespoons of oil and continue to cook the eggplants for 4 to 5 minutes on each side or until soft. You may need to add a little extra oil. Do this in two batches.

Remove from the pan, allow to cool, then place in a food processor with the garlic and herbs. Blend for 1 to 2 minutes or until a purée is formed then add sufficient of the remaining oil to give a very soft consistency. Scrape into a bowl, stir in the Parmesan cheese and seasoning to taste, cover, and leave in the refrigerator until required.

Meanwhile wipe the lamb steaks and place in a shallow dish. Blend the oil, lemon juice, and herbs together and pour over the lamb. Cover loosely and leave in the refrigerator for 30 minutes. Turn the steaks at least once during this time.

When ready to cook the lamb, lightly brush or spray your grill pan again with oil, heat on a moderate heat until hot.

Remove the lamb from the marinade and cook in the pan for 4 to 5 minutes each side or until done to personal preference.

Serve the lamb steaks with the polenta and the prepared Eggplant Pesto. Garnish with basil sprigs.

Serves **4**
Preparation time **15 minutes**
   plus 30 minutes marinating time
Cooking time **28 to 32 minutes**

FOR THE PESTO
1 small eggplant (about 8 oz in weight)
Salt
6 to 8 Tbsp olive oil
4 garlic cloves, peeled and crushed
2 Tbsp chopped fresh mint
1 Tbsp chopped fresh parsley
4 Tbsp grated Parmesan cheese
Salt and freshly ground black pepper

FOR THE LAMB
Four 5-oz lamb leg steaks
2 Tbsp olive oil
4 Tbsp lemon juice
2 Tbsp chopped fresh parsley
1 Tbsp chopped fresh mint
1 Tbsp chopped fresh basil

TO SERVE
Polenta *(see page 104)*

TO GARNISH
Basil sprigs

SPICED LAMB KABOBS
WITH COUSCOUS

WHEN BUYING COUSCOUS, LOOK FOR THE INSTANT VARIETY.

Serves **4**
Preparation time **8 minutes plus 30 minutes marinating time**
Cooking time **11 to 13 minutes, including the couscous**

1 Tbsp ground cumin
1 tsp ground coriander
1 tsp ground cinnamon
1½ tsp ground ginger
1 Tbsp lemon juice
1 lb boneless lamb, trimmed
2 medium red onions, peeled and cut into wedges
16 fresh bay leaves

FOR THE COUSCOUS
1¼ cups couscous
A few strands saffron
1 tsp ground cinnamon
2 tsp butter
1 carrot, peeled and grated
½ cup raisins
Freshly milled salt to taste, optional

TO SERVE
Assorted salad leaves

Blend the spices to a paste with the lemon juice then spread over the lamb. Cover lightly and leave in the refrigerator for 30 minutes then cut into bite-size cubes.

Thread the lamb, red onion, and bay leaves alternately onto eight small wooden skewers.

Lightly brush or spray your grill pan with oil then place on a moderate heat until hot. Cook the lamb for 6 to 8 minutes, turning occasionally, or until done to personal preference.

Meanwhile place the couscous in a bowl with the saffron and pour over 1¼ cups of boiling water to cover. Leave for 5 minutes, forking occasionally, until the grains have absorbed the water. Stir in the ground cinnamon, butter, carrot, and raisins with salt to taste if using.

Serve the kabobs on a bed of couscous with assorted salad leaves.

Spiced Lamb Kabobs with Couscous

LAMB STEAKS WITH
GINGER AND CILANTRO

THIS MAKES A PERFECT MIDWEEK DISH, EASY TO PREPARE AND
QUICK TO COOK. CHOOSE STEAKS THAT ARE REASONABLY THIN
SO THEY COOK QUICKLY.

Serves **4**
Preparation time **4 minutes plus**
  30 minutes marinating time
Cooking time **6 to 10 minutes**

One 2-in piece gingerroot, peeled and
  grated fine
2 Tbsp chopped fresh cilantro
4 garlic cloves, peeled and crushed
1 Tbsp grated orange zest
2 tsp liquid honey, warmed
1 Tbsp orange juice
Four 5-oz lamb leg steaks

TO GARNISH
Cilantro sprigs

TO SERVE
Freshly cooked pasta noodles, tossed in
  orange zest, freshly chopped cilantro,
  and a little oil; green salad

Blend together the ginger, cilantro, garlic, orange zest, honey, and orange juice,
and brush over both sides of the lamb steaks. Leave the steaks, lightly covered,
in a shallow dish in the refrigerator for 30 minutes.

Lightly brush or spray your grill pan with oil then place on a moderate heat
until hot.

Cook the lamb steaks in the pan for 3 to 5 minutes each side or until done to
personal preference.

Garnish with cilantro sprigs and serve with the cooked noodles and a crisp
green salad.

PEPPERED LAMB WITH
APPLE CROSTINI

THESE CROSTINI ARE AN IDEAL CHOICE FOR A SUMMER LUNCH. IF YOU PREFER NOT TO MAKE YOUR OWN MAYONNAISE, STIR SOME CHOPPED FRESH MINT INTO GOOD-QUALITY READY-MADE MAYONNAISE.

Blend the olive oil, apple juice, and honey then pour over the lamb and add the mint sprigs. Cover lightly and leave in the refrigerator for 30 minutes. Spoon the marinade over occasionally. Remove from the marinade and roll in the crushed peppercorns.

Lightly brush or spray your grill pan with oil then place on a moderate heat until hot. Cook the lamb for 3 to 5 minutes, stirring occasionally, or until done to personal preference. Remove from the pan and drain off any juices. Keep warm.

Brush the apple rings with the butter then cook in the grill pan for 2 minutes each side or until golden. Remove and keep warm.

Toast the French bread in the grill pan for 1 to 2 minutes.

Arrange the salad leaves on the toasted bread, top with the cooked lamb and the apple rings. Sprinkle with black pepper and serve with a spoonful of mint mayonnaise.

Serves **4**
Preparation time
  8 minutes plus 30 minutes marinating time
Cooking time **6 to 9 minutes**

2 Tbsp olive oil
⅔ cup apple juice
2 tsp liquid honey, warmed
1 lb boneless lean lamb, cut into thin strips
A few mint sprigs
2 Tbsp crushed pink or mixed peppercorns

1 baking apple, peeled, cored, and cut into rings
1 Tbsp melted sweet butter
4 wedges French bread, split in half

TO SERVE
Bitter salad leaves, freshly ground black pepper, and mint-flavored mayonnaise

LAMB FILLET WITH
PLUM SAUCE

DARK RED PLUMS WORK BEST IN THIS PLUM SAUCE AND, FOR MAXIMUM FLAVOR, MAKE SURE THEY ARE AS RIPE AS POSSIBLE.

Serves **4**
Preparation time
  8 minutes plus 30 minutes
  marinating time
Cooking time **20 to 25 minutes**

1½ lb lamb fillet
2 Tbsp hoisin sauce
4 Tbsp plum preserves
2 Tbsp oil
3 Tbsp light soy sauce

FOR THE PLUM SAUCE
10 oz fresh plums, rinsed
  and pitted
2 shallots, peeled and chopped
2 Tbsp dark soft brown sugar
2 Tbsp red wine vinegar

TO SERVE
Freshly cooked egg noodles
  tossed with chopped scallions,
  chopped radishes, and
  chopped flat-leaf parsley

Trim the lamb, cut into three pieces, and place in a shallow dish. Heat the hoisin sauce, plum preserves, oil, and soy sauce and stir until smooth. Brush over the lamb fillet and leave, lightly covered, in the refrigerator for 30 minutes.

Meanwhile place the plums, shallots, sugar, and vinegar in a pan and cook gently for 12 to 15 minutes or until the plums are done. Pass through a food processor and, if a smooth sauce is preferred, rub through a sieve. Warm gently just before serving.

Lightly brush or spray your grill pan with oil then place on a moderate heat until hot. Cook the lamb fillet in the pan for 8 to 10 minutes, turning occasionally, or until done to personal preference.

Slice then serve on top of the noodles with the sauce on the side.

LAMB WITH GREEN OLIVE
TAPENADE

LAMB IS BEST EATEN SLIGHTLY PINK BUT IF PREFERRED, COOK THE NOISETTES FOR A LITTLE LONGER, TAKING CARE NOT TO OVERCOOK THEM.

Serves **4**
Preparation time **8 minutes**
Cooking time **6 to 10 minutes**

8 lamb noisettes
2 Tbsp pitted green olives, cut
  into thin slivers
2 large garlic cloves, peeled and
  cut into thin slivers

FOR THE TAPENADE
2 garlic cloves, peeled and
  crushed
2 Tbsp capers, drained

¾ cup pitted green olives
One 2-oz can anchovy fillets,
  drained
½ cup olive oil
1 Tbsp lemon juice
1 Tbsp chopped fresh parsley

TO SERVE
Mashed potatoes flavored with
  chopped scallions and grilled
  fennel (slice two fennel bulbs
  then cook in the preheated
  grill pan for 6 to 8 minutes or
  until tender)

Wipe the noisettes and if necessary secure with fine twine to ensure they keep their shape during cooking. Using a sharp knife make small slits in the surface of the lamb and insert the slivers of green olive and garlic. Set aside.

Place all the ingredients for the Tapenade in a food processor and blend for 1 minute. Scrape into a bowl and set aside.

Lightly brush or spray your grill pan with oil then place on a moderate heat until hot. Add the lamb noisettes and cook for 3 to 5 minutes each side or until done to personal preference.

Serve on a bed of scallion-flavored mashed potatoes with the grilled fennel and hand the prepared Green Olive Tapenade separately.

HERBED LAMB AND
MUSTARD BURGERS

EVERYONE HAS THEIR OWN FAVORITE MUSTARD. FOR A REAL BITE, TRY MIXING YOUR OWN USING DRIED MUSTARD POWDER. ONCE BLENDED WITH WATER, THIS IS FAR HOTTER THAN ANY READY-MADE VARIETY.

Place all the ingredients for the burgers in a mixing bowl and mix together, binding with the beaten egg. Place on a chopping board and with slightly dampened hands form into four burgers. Place on a plate, cover lightly, and leave in the refrigerator for 30 minutes.

Lightly brush or spray your grill pan with oil then place on a moderate heat until hot. Cook the burgers for 4 to 5 minutes each side or until done to personal preference. Serve on warm naan bread or on a bed of tomato rice pilaf with a crisp green salad, and hand the yogurt separately. Garnish with chopped fresh herbs.

Serves **4**
Preparation time **10 to 12 minutes**
  plus 30 minutes chilling time
Cooking time **8 to 10 minutes**

1 lb ground lamb
1 to 1½ Tbsp whole-grain mustard
1 medium red onion, peeled and
  chopped fine
3 garlic cloves, peeled and crushed
½ cup raisins
Salt and freshly ground black
  pepper
2 Tbsp chopped fresh oregano
1 small egg, beaten

TO SERVE
Warm naan bread or tomato rice
  pilaf; crisp green salad; and
  low-fat, plain yogurt

TO GARNISH
Chopped fresh herbs

PORK

SEVILLE-MARINATED PORK

FRESH SAGE ADDS A SUBTLE FLAVOR AND COLOR TO MANY DISHES
AND COMBINES PARTICULARLY WELL WITH PORK.

Serves **4**

Preparation time **5 minutes plus 30 minutes marinating time**

Cooking time **13 to 15 minutes**

Four 4-oz boneless pork chops

4 Tbsp Seville orange marmalade

2 Tbsp finely grated fresh ginger or 2 tsp ground ginger

3 Tbsp lemon juice

2 Tbsp dark soy sauce

⅔ cup orange juice

TO GARNISH

Fresh sage leaves and charred orange wedges

TO SERVE

Freshly cooked new potatoes and stir-fried vegetables

Trim the pork chops of any excess fat and wipe. Place in a shallow dish and set aside. Stir the orange marmalade with the ginger, the lemon juice, and soy sauce over a moderate heat until blended then pour over the chops. Cover lightly then leave in the refrigerator for 30 minutes.

Lightly brush or spray your grill pan with oil then place on a moderate heat until hot. Drain the pork chops and cook in the pan for 4 to 5 minutes each side or until done.

Add the orange juice to the pan juices and heat gently for 5 minutes, carefully swirling the juices together, and pour over the chops.

Garnish with sage leaves and orange wedges and serve with the freshly cooked vegetables.

PORK AND ZUCCHINI KABOBS

SUN-DRIED TOMATOES PROVIDE AN INTENSE TOMATO FLAVOR.

Serves **4**

Preparation time
  8 minutes plus 30 minutes marinating time

Cooking time **7 to 9 minutes**

1 lb pork fillet

2 Tbsp sun-dried tomatoes, chopped

6 Tbsp olive oil

4 Tbsp lemon juice

2 Tbsp chopped fresh oregano

8 oz zucchini, trimmed and cut into bite-size pieces

TO GARNISH

Oregano sprigs

TO SERVE

Chunks of warm Italian-style bread, and Chargrilled Vegetables with Green Olives *(see page 103)*

Cut the pork into bite-size pieces and place in a shallow dish. Cover the sun-dried tomatoes with boiling water and allow to soak for 5 minutes. Drain, then place in a food processor with the olive oil and lemon juice and blend until a thick paste is formed. Stir in the chopped oregano and pour over the pork. Cover lightly and leave in the refrigerator for at least 30 minutes, either turning the pork occasionally or spooning over the marinade.

When ready to cook drain the pork and thread alternately with the zucchini onto eight small wooden skewers.

Lightly brush or spray your grill pan with oil then place on a moderate heat until hot. Cook the kabobs in the pan, turning occasionally, for 7 to 9 minutes or until done.

Garnish with fresh oregano sprigs and serve with the warm bread and the Chargrilled Vegetables with Green Olives.

PORK NOISETTES WITH
PRUNES AND CHESTNUTS

PEELING FRESH CHESTNUTS CAN BE HARD WORK BUT THIS METHOD WORKS
EVERY TIME. IF YOU PREFER, USE READY-PEELED, COOKED CHESTNUTS,
AVAILABLE FROM MOST SUPERMARKETS.

Wipe the noisettes and if necessary secure with fine twine or toothpicks to ensure the noisettes keep a good shape. Place in a shallow dish and scatter over the prunes.

Mix together the red wine with the broth, honey, and vinegar and pour over the noisettes and prunes. Cover lightly and leave in the refrigerator for 30 minutes.

Make a slit at the top of the chestnuts then boil for 10 minutes. Drain and dry thoroughly.

Lightly brush or spray your grill pan with oil then place on a moderate heat until hot. Add the chestnuts and cook for 10 to 15 minutes or until the skins begin to open. Remove from heat, allow to cool, then peel. Set aside.

When ready to cook, lightly brush or spray the grill pan and heat as above then add 1 tablespoon of the oil. Drain the noisettes, reserving the marinade, and cook in the pan over a moderate heat for 4 to 6 minutes on each side or until done, adding the extra oil if the pan becomes dry.

Meanwhile place the marinade in a small pan and boil vigorously until reduced by half then stir in the chestnuts. Garnish the noisettes and serve with the vegetables, chestnuts, and sauce.

Serves **4**
Preparation time **15 minutes plus
30 minutes marinating time**
Cooking time **30 to 39 minutes**

8 small pork noisettes
½ cup ready-to-eat prunes, chopped
⅔ cup red wine
⅔ cup chicken or vegetable broth
1 Tbsp liquid honey
2 Tbsp balsamic vinegar
½ cup chestnuts
1 to 2 Tbsp sunflower oil

TO GARNISH
**Fresh rosemary sprigs and freshly ground
black pepper**

TO SERVE
**Mustard-flavored mashed potatoes and
freshly cooked baby vegetables**

PORK STEAKS WITH APRICOT

FRUIT GOES WELL WITH PORK, AND APRICOTS ARE
A PARTICULARLY SUCCESSFUL COMBINATION.

Serves **4**
Preparation time
  5 minutes plus 30 minutes
  marinating time
Cooking time **13 to 15 minutes**

One 14-oz can apricots in natural
  juice
2 Tbsp white wine vinegar
Four 5-oz pork steaks
2 cinnamon sticks, broken in half

2 Tbsp light soft brown sugar
1 to 2 Tbsp sunflower oil
2 Tbsp butter

TO GARNISH
Fresh herbs and fresh sliced
  apricots

TO SERVE
White and wild rice and freshly
  cooked sugar snap peas

Drain the apricots, reserving ⅔ cup of the juice, then purée the
apricots and mix with the apricot juice and white wine vinegar.

Trim the steaks if necessary, wipe, place in a shallow dish and
scatter over the cinnamon sticks, then pour over the apricot
purée. Cover lightly and leave in the refrigerator for 30 minutes.

When ready to cook, lightly brush or spray your grill pan with
oil then place on a moderate heat until hot. Add 1 tablespoon
of the oil. Drain the steaks, pour the marinade into a small pan,
and add the sugar. Gently boil with the cinnamon sticks for
2 minutes. Reduce the heat, add the butter, and simmer for
3 minutes, stirring occasionally. Keep warm. Discard cinnamon
sticks before use.

Meanwhile cook the steaks in the hot grill pan for 4 to 5 minutes
each side or until done, adding the extra oil if required.

Garnish and serve with the sauce, rice, and sugar snap peas.

PORK WITH ARTICHOKES AND BLACK OLIVES

THESE ROULADES OF PORK ARE WICKEDLY GOOD.
THE COMBINATION OF THE INGREDIENTS WORKS
EXCEPTIONALLY WELL AND PROVIDES A MEAL
THAT'S FIT FOR A KING.

Serves **4**
Preparation time
  12 to 15 minutes
Cooking time **10 to 12 minutes**

Four 4-oz pork escalopes
½ cup canned artichoke hearts,
  drained
½ cup pitted black olives
4 slices Parma ham
4 slices mozzarella cheese
A few sprigs fresh basil

TO SERVE
Freshly cooked noodles tossed in
  2 Tbsp melted butter and a few
  chopped olives; and an
  artichoke and tomato salad

TO GARNISH
Fresh basil sprigs

Place the pork escalopes between two sheets of waxed paper
and pound with a meat mallet until ¼-inch thick. Set aside.

Place the artichoke hearts and olives in a food processor and
blend to a thick paste. Spread thinly over one side of the meat.

Lay a slice of Parma ham and then a slice of mozzarella and
2 to 3 basil leaves on top of the meat. Roll up and secure with
either fine twine or toothpicks.

Lightly brush or spray your grill pan with oil then place on a
moderate heat until hot. Add the pork and cook, turning
occasionally, for 10 to 12 minutes or until done. Remove from the
pan, discard the twine or toothpicks, and if you like, slice to serve
with cooked noodles and salad and garnished with basil sprigs.

ORIENTAL-STYLE PORK BITES

NORMALLY WHEN YOU USE WOODEN SKEWERS IT IS OVER A BARBECUE OR UNDER A BROILER AND YOU NEED TO SOAK THE SKEWERS IN COLD WATER FOR 30 MINUTES. IT IS ENTIRELY UP TO YOU IF YOU DO THIS WHEN USING THEM IN YOUR GRILL PAN, BUT AFTER TESTING I DISCOVERED THAT IT REALLY WAS NOT NECESSARY.

Place the pork into a shallow dish and set aside. Blend the sugar with the soy sauce, plum sauce, and sherry. Stir in the ginger and the lightly crushed star anise and pour over the pork. Cover and leave in the refrigerator for 30 minutes. Stir occasionally during marinating.

Drain the pork and thread with pieces of celery and onion wedges onto eight small wooden skewers. Lightly brush or spray your grill pan with oil then place on a moderate heat until hot. Cook the pork kabobs for 8 to 10 minutes, turning frequently, until done.

Garnish with fresh herbs and serve with rice or noodles and the stir-fried vegetables.

Serves **4**
Preparation time **8 minutes plus**
  30 minutes marinating time
Cooking time **8 to 10 minutes**

12 oz lean pork, cubed
1 Tbsp dark soft brown sugar
3 Tbsp light soy sauce
2 Tbsp Thai plum sauce
2 Tbsp medium-dry sherry
1 Tbsp grated fresh ginger
3 to 4 star anise, lightly crushed
2 celery stalks, trimmed and cut into
  bite-size pieces
1 medium red onion, peeled and cut into
  wedges

TO GARNISH
Fresh herbs

TO SERVE
Steamed rice or noodles and
  stir-fried vegetables

ALMOND-STUFFED PORK

THIS MAKES AN IMPRESSIVE DINNER PARTY DISH. TAKE CARE THAT YOU LOWER THE HEAT UNDER THE FILLET SO THAT YOU DO NOT BURN THE OUTSIDE. ROLL ANY EXTRA STUFFING INTO SMALL BALLS AND COOK IN THE PAN FOR THE LAST FEW MINUTES OF THE PORK COOKING TIME.

Trim the pork of any excess fat then, using a sharp knife, make a slit along one side of the fillet. Set aside.

Heat the oil in a pan and gently sauté the shallots and garlic for 5 minutes. Remove from the heat and stir in the almonds, apple, raisins, orange zest, bread crumbs, and thyme. Season to taste then bind with the egg and orange juice to form a stiff consistency.

Use the mixture to stuff the pork fillet. Wrap the bacon slices around the pork, securing with either fine twine or toothpicks.

Lightly brush or spray your grill pan with oil then place on a moderate heat until hot. Cook the fillet in the pan for 10 minutes, turning occasionally. Reduce the heat and continue to cook, turning occasionally, for 20 to 25 minutes or until done.

Discard the twine or toothpicks, slice, garnish, and serve with buttered new potatoes and chargrilled tomatoes.

Serves **4**
Preparation time **15 minutes**
Cooking time **35 to 40 minutes**

One 1 lb-piece pork fillet
1 Tbsp oil
2 shallots, peeled and chopped
2 to 3 garlic cloves, peeled and crushed
6 Tbsp ground almonds
1 crisp apple, peeled, cored, and chopped fine
½ cup raisins
1 Tbsp grated orange zest
1 cup fresh bread crumbs
2 Tbsp chopped fresh thyme
Salt and freshly ground black pepper
1 medium egg, beaten
2 Tbsp orange juice
6 bacon slices

TO GARNISH
Thyme sprigs and orange wedges

TO SERVE
Buttered new potatoes or chargrilled tomatoes on the vine with olive oil and coarse salt

CAJUN PORK WITH COUSCOUS

WHEN USING PISTACHIO NUTS IN COOKING AVOID THE
READY-SALTED ONES.

Serves **4**

Preparation time
**10 to 12 minutes plus 30
minutes marinating time**

Cooking time **8 to 10 minutes**

12 oz lean pork such as fillet
2 garlic cloves, peeled and crushed
**1 to 2 red serrano chillies, seeded and
chopped**
1 Tbsp Cajun seasoning mix
⅔ cup tomato juice

FOR THE COUSCOUS

1 cup couscous
**2 ripe tomatoes, skinned, seeded, and
chopped**
4 scallions, trimmed and chopped
**½ to 1 tsp crushed dried chillies,
optional**
½ cup raisins
**½ cup pistachio nuts, shelled and
chopped**
1 tsp ground coriander
1 tsp ground cumin
3 Tbsp lemon juice
2 Tbsp olive oil
2 Tbsp chopped fresh thyme

TO GARNISH

Fresh thyme

Trim the pork, cut into bite-size pieces, and place in a shallow dish. Blend the
garlic, chillies, Cajun seasoning, and tomato juice and pour over the pork.
Cover and leave in the refrigerator, stirring occasionally, for 30 minutes.

Drain the pork and thread onto eight small wooden skewers. Lightly brush or
spray your grill pan with oil then place on a moderate heat until hot. Cook the
kabobs for 8 to 10 minutes, turning occasionally, or until done.

Meanwhile place the couscous in a heatproof bowl and cover with boiling water.
Leave until the water is absorbed, stirring occasionally. Stir in the remaining
ingredients and mix lightly. Arrange the couscous on plates, place the kabobs
on top, garnish, and serve.

Cajun Pork with Couscous

SPICE-CRUSTED PORK BROCHETTES

THESE BROCHETTES WORK WELL WITH CARDAMOM-FLAVORED RICE. MAKE SURE TO USE FRESH CARDAMOM PODS. LIGHTLY POUND THEM TO CRACK THE HUSKS.

Serves **4**
Preparation time **5 to 8 minutes plus 30 minutes marinating time**
Cooking time **12 to 15 minutes**

10 oz lean pork such as fillet
⅔ cup low-fat, plain yogurt
4 Tbsp lemon juice
1 tsp harissa, or chili powder, or to taste
1 Tbsp ground cumin
1½ tsp ground coriander
1 tsp paprika
1 tsp ground ginger
1 tsp ground cinnamon
2 small bell peppers (use different colors), seeded and cut into wedges, or 1 large bell pepper
1 large onion, peeled and cut into wedges

TO SERVE
Yogurt and Cucumber Dip *(see page 17)*, **cardamom-flavored rice, warm pita bread, and crisp green salad leaves**

Trim the pork fillet, cut into bite-size pieces, and place in a shallow dish. Blend the yogurt with the lemon juice and spices then pour over the pork. Cover lightly and leave in the refrigerator for 30 minutes, occasionally spooning over the marinade.

Drain the pork and thread alternately with the bell pepper and onion wedges onto eight small wooden skewers.

Lightly brush or spray your grill pan with oil then place on a moderate heat until hot. Cook the brochettes for 12 to 15 minutes or until the pork is done, turning frequently.

Serve with the Yogurt and Cucumber Dip, rice, warm pita bread, and salad.

PAN-FRIED PORK WITH
CHARRED APPLE RELISH

WHILE FRESH CRANBERRIES ARE SOUR, DRIED ONES ARE SWEET BUT STILL
RETAIN A CERTAIN TARTNESS WHICH WORKS WELL WITH PORK. YOU CAN SUBSTITUTE
WITH RAISINS IF DRIED CRANBERRIES ARE NOT AVAILABLE.

Trim the escalopes if necessary, wipe, and place in a shallow dish. Blend the mustard with the apple juice and pour over the escalopes. Scatter with the sage leaves, cover lightly, and leave in the refrigerator for 30 minutes.

Lightly brush or spray your grill pan with oil then place on a moderate heat until hot. Add the apple pieces and cook for 2 to 3 minutes or until soft but not pulpy and slightly charred. Remove from the pan and add to the remaining relish ingredients, stir, and set aside.

Drain the escalopes and cook in the hot pan for 3 to 5 minutes each side or until the pork is done.

Slice the pork and place on a bed of spinach leaves. Serve with the Apple Relish, potatoes, and freshly cooked vegetables. Garnish with sage leaves.

Serves **4**
Preparation time **8 minutes plus 30 minutes marinating time**
Cooking time **8 to 13 minutes**

Four 4-oz pork escalopes
2 tsp whole-grain mustard
$\frac{2}{3}$ cup clear apple juice
A few fresh sage leaves, lightly crushed

FOR THE RELISH
8 oz apples, peeled, cored, and chopped fine
2 Tbsp dried cranberries or raisins
1 Tbsp cider vinegar
1 tsp whole-grain mustard
$\frac{2}{3}$ cup sour cream

TO SERVE
Spinach leaves, sautéed potatoes, freshly cooked baby carrots, sugar snap peas

TO GARNISH
Deep-fried sage leaves

SWEET-AND-SOUR PORK

THIS RECIPE ALSO WORKS WELL WITH SPARE RIBS.

Trim the escalopes if necessary, wipe, and place in a shallow dish. Blend the tomato paste with the sherry, vinegar, honey, pineapple juice, and soy sauce. Pour over the pork, cover lightly, and leave in the refrigerator for 30 minutes.

Lightly brush or spray your grill pan with oil then place on a moderate heat until hot. Drain the escalopes, reserving the marinade. Cook the escalopes in the hot grill pan for 6 to 8 minutes or until thoroughly done. Remove from the pan and set aside.

Meanwhile boil the marinade vigorously for 3 minutes then reduce the heat, add the carrot and celery, and simmer for 2 minutes. Blend the cornstarch with 2 tablespoons of either pineapple juice or water then stir into the sauce and cook, stirring for 1 minute or until thickened.

Add the cucumber and heat for 1 minute, then slice the pork escalopes and serve with the rice and salad sprinkled with toasted sesame seeds.

Serves **4**
Preparation time **10 minutes plus 30 minutes marinating time**
Cooking time **13 to 15 minutes**

Four 5-oz pork escalopes
2 Tbsp tomato paste
2 Tbsp medium-dry sherry
3 Tbsp white wine vinegar
1 to 2 tsp liquid honey, warmed
1¼ cups pineapple juice
2 Tbsp dark soy sauce
1 small carrot, peeled and cut into matchstick strips
1 celery stalk, trimmed and cut into matchstick strips
1 Tbsp cornstarch
One 2-in piece cucumber, cut into matchstick strips

TO SERVE
Freshly cooked rice and tossed green salad with sliced raw mushrooms

TO GARNISH
Toasted sesame seeds

POULTRY

CARIBBEAN CHICKEN WITH
WARM FRUIT SALSA

SALSAS ARE VERY POPULAR AND CAN BE MADE USING MANY DIFFERENT INGREDIENTS. THE CHILLIES
IN THIS SALSA GIVE IT A PLEASANT FIERY TANG. USE AS MUCH CHILI AS YOUR PALATE CAN TAKE.

Make three slashes diagonally across each chicken breast and place in a shallow dish.

Blend the garlic, chili, lime zest, and ginger then stir in the fruit juices and cilantro. Pour over the chicken breasts, cover lightly, and leave in the refrigerator for 30 minutes, occasionally spooning the marinade over.

Meanwhile lightly brush or spray your grill pan with oil then place on a moderate heat until hot. Slice the papaya thickly. Pat the fruit dry on paper towels. Place the fruits in the grill pan and cook for 1 to 2 minutes each side until seared. Remove, chop fine, and mix with remaining salsa ingredients. Place in a small pan and heat gently just before serving.

Heat the grill pan again, add the oil, then drain the chicken pieces. Cook in the grill pan for 5 to 6 minutes each side or until done. Garnish and serve, sitting on 1 to 2 spoonfuls of warm Salsa, with grilled tomatoes, rice, and a crisp green salad.

Serves **4**
Preparation time **10 minutes plus 30 minutes marinating time**
Cooking time **12 to 16 minutes**

4 boneless, skinless chicken breasts
2 large garlic cloves, peeled and crushed
½ to 1 habanero chili, seeded and chopped fine
1 Tbsp grated lime zest
2 Tbsp grated fresh ginger
3 Tbsp lime juice
½ cup mango or orange juice
2 Tbsp chopped fresh cilantro
1 Tbsp sunflower oil

FOR THE SALSA

1 firm but ripe papaya, peeled and seeded
1 small or 2 to 3 slices fresh pineapple, peeled and sliced
2 firm tomatoes, seeded and chopped
4 scallions, trimmed and chopped fine
2 Tbsp chopped fresh cilantro

TO GARNISH

Chopped fresh cilantro and lime wedges

TO SERVE

Grilled tomatoes, rice, and crisp green salad

HOISIN ROCK CORNISH HENS

ROCK CORNISH GAME HENS NEED TO BE THOROUGHLY COOKED. FOR THIS REASON, IT IS BEST TO BUY SMALLER BIRDS.

Cut the birds into quarters and remove the backbone completely. Make a few slashes across the joints piercing right through to the bone. (This will help to ensure that the birds are thoroughly cooked.) Lightly rinse the joints, pat dry, and place in a large shallow dish.

Blend all the other ingredients together and pour over the bird quarters. Cover loosely and leave in the refrigerator for 30 minutes, occasionally spooning the marinade over.

Lightly brush or spray your grill pan with oil then place on a moderate heat until hot. When ready to cook, drain the quarters, reserving the marinade, and cook in the grill pan, skin-side down, for 3 minutes. Turn the quarters over and continue to cook for a further 12 to 15 minutes or until cooked through. The juices should run clear when you pierce the meat with a knife. Press the quarters down with a spatula occasionally to help with the cooking.

Meanwhile boil the marinade ingredients for 3 minutes. Remove the hens from the pan, arrange on plates, and garnish. Serve with the hot marinade, the noodles, and the Oriental Salad.

Serves **4**
Preparation time **10 minutes plus 30 minutes marinating time**
Cooking time **18 to 21 minutes**

4 small or 2 large rock Cornish hens
2 Tbsp freshly grated fresh ginger
3 Tbsp hoisin sauce
1 Tbsp liquid honey, warmed
3 Tbsp light soy sauce
2 Tbsp medium-dry sherry
1 Tbsp sunflower oil
2 Tbsp grated orange zest
⅔ cup orange juice

TO GARNISH
Orange wedges, strips of orange zest, and flat-leaf parsley

TO SERVE
Freshly cooked noodles, tossed with grated orange zest and chopped parsley, and Oriental Salad
(see page 102)

PAN-FRIED CHICKEN WITH TARRAGON

CHICKEN AND TARRAGON IS A CLASSIC COMBINATION. USE FRESH TARRAGON AND CHOP JUST BEFORE USE.

Wipe the chicken breasts and make a few slits in each. Insert a few tarragon leaves in the slits and set aside.

Lightly brush or spray your grill pan with oil then place on a moderate heat until hot. Add the butter and when melted add the chicken and cook for 5 to 6 minutes each side or until done. Remove from the pan and set aside.

Add the wine and shallots to the pan and bring to a boil, boil for 2 minutes, then reduce the heat and stir in the cream. Boil gently for 1 minute or until the sauce has thickened slightly. Stir in the tarragon with seasoning to taste, heat for 1 minute, then serve with the cooked chicken and vegetables.

Serves **4**
Preparation time **5 minutes**
Cooking time **16 to 18 minutes**

4 boneless, skinless chicken breasts
A few sprigs fresh tarragon
1 Tbsp unsalted butter
1 cup medium-dry white wine
2 shallots, peeled and fine chopped
⅔ cup heavy cream
2 Tbsp chopped fresh tarragon
Salt and freshly ground black pepper

TO SERVE
Freshly cooked baby potatoes and baby vegetables

YOGURT CHICKEN WITH
MINT DRESSING

THE LONGER YOU LEAVE THE CHICKEN MARINATING, THE STRONGER
THE FLAVOR, AND THIS APPLIES TO ALL FOOD BEING MARINATED.
IF TIME PERMITS, TRY MARINATING OVERNIGHT.

Serves **4**

Preparation time **10 minutes plus
30 minutes marinating time**

Cooking time **12 to 14 minutes**

4 boneless, skinless chicken breasts
1 red serrano chili, seeded and chopped
3 garlic cloves, peeled and crushed
1 Tbsp grated fresh ginger
1 Tbsp grated lemon zest
1 Tbsp paprika
3 Tbsp lemon juice
⅔ cup plain yogurt
2 Tbsp chopped fresh cilantro

FOR THE MINT DRESSING
⅔ cup plain yogurt
1 Tbsp grated lemon zest
2 Tbsp chopped fresh mint

TO SERVE
**Shredded lettuce, watercress,
    or arugula and sliced red onion salad;
    warm naan bread; freshly cooked
    basmati or wild rice**

Wipe the chicken breasts and make three diagonal slashes across each breast.
Place in a shallow dish.

Blend together the chili, garlic, ginger, lemon zest, and paprika then stir in the
lemon juice and yogurt. Pour over the chicken breasts, cover lightly, and leave
for 30 minutes in the refrigerator to allow the flavors to permeate the chicken.

Meanwhile blend together the ingredients for the dressing, cover, and leave in
the refrigerator until required.

When ready to cook, lightly brush or spray your grill pan with oil then place
on a moderate heat until hot. Drain the chicken and cook in the grill pan for
6 to 7 minutes each side or until done. Sprinkle with the chopped cilantro.

Serve with the dressing on the side, with the salad, rice, and naan bread.

Maple-glazed Turkey

MAPLE-GLAZED TURKEY

THESE KABOBS ARE EQUALLY DELICIOUS EATEN HOT OR COLD.
MAKE MORE THAN YOU NEED AND KEEP FOR A COUPLE OF DAYS
IN THE REFRIGERATOR FOR UNEXPECTED VISITORS.

Serves **4**

Preparation time **8 minutes plus**
  30 minutes marinating time

Cooking time **14 to 16 minutes**

1 lb fresh turkey breast

2 Tbsp maple syrup

2 Tbsp tomato paste

1 Tbsp Worcestershire sauce

1 tsp ready-made whole-grain mustard

3 Tbsp lemon juice

1 Tbsp sunflower oil

2 medium ripe but firm plantains,
  peeled, sliced into rounds

1 ripe mango, peeled, pitted, and sliced

TO SERVE

Slices of Italian-style bread such as
  focaccia, a few spinach leaves, tough
  stems removed and rinsed, guacamole

TO GARNISH

Fresh snipped chives

Cut the turkey into thin strips and place in a shallow dish. Blend the maple syrup
with the tomato paste, Worcestershire sauce, mustard, and lemon juice and
pour over the turkey. Cover loosely and leave for 30 minutes in the refrigerator,
stirring occasionally. Drain and thread onto eight skewers.

Lightly brush or spray your grill pan with oil then place on a moderate heat until
hot. Add the oil and cook the plantains and mango for 5 minutes, turning at least
once, or until softened and lightly charred. Remove from the pan and keep warm.

Drain the turkey and cook for 8 to 10 minutes or until done, turning frequently.
(Add a little extra oil if the turkey is sticking to the pan.) Remove from the pan
and keep warm. Add the bread slices to the pan and cook for 1 minute each side.

Arrange the spinach leaves on top of the bread, top with the turkey, garnish, and
serve with the mango, plantains, and the guacamole.

DUCK BREASTS WITH
WARM MANGO SALSA

DUCK BREASTS ARE BEST SERVED SLIGHTLY PINK. MAKE THREE SLASHES ACROSS THE BREASTS
TO HELP THEM COOK QUICKER.

Wipe the duck breasts, make three deep diagonal slashes across the skin on each breast, and place in a shallow dish. Blend the fruit juice, soy sauce, and honey then pour over the duck breasts. Cover lightly and leave in the refrigerator for at least 30 minutes, spooning the marinade over occasionally.

Combine all the ingredients for the salsa except the cilantro, place in a small pan, and set aside.

When ready to cook, lightly brush or spray your grill pan with oil then place on a moderate heat until hot. Drain the duck breasts and cook, skin-side down, in the pan for 4 minutes, then turn and continue to cook over a moderate heat for 12 minutes or until done to personal preference. Remove from the pan and keep warm.

Drain off any excess fat, leaving about 2 tablespoons in the pan. Add the cubed butternut squash and baby corn and cook for about 5 minutes, or until soft, keeping the vegetables moving constantly. Stir in the scallions.

At the same time, place the Salsa over a moderate heat and heat gently for 5 minutes, then stir in the chopped cilantro.

Arrange the duck breasts on warm serving plates with the Salsa and butternut squash mixture. Garnish with the corn salad and strips of beet.

Serves **4**
Preparation time
  10 to 12 minutes, plus 30 minutes marinating time
Cooking time **26 minutes**

4 duck breasts
⅔ cup mango or orange juice
2 Tbsp light soy sauce
2 tsp liquid honey, warmed

FOR THE SALSA
1 small ripe mango, peeled, pitted, and diced fine
4 scallions, trimmed and chopped fine
1 small red onion, peeled and chopped fine
1 to 2 tsp dark soft brown sugar
½ to 1 tsp hot chili sauce, or to taste
2 Tbsp chopped fresh cilantro

TO SERVE
8 oz butternut squash, peeled, seeded, and cubed
6 oz baby corn
6 scallions, trimmed and diagonally sliced

TO GARNISH
Corn salad with thin strips of raw beet

GARLIC TURKEY

COOKED IN THIS WAY, GARLIC IS CREAMY AND NOT PUNGENT. IT CAN THEN BE EASILY SPREAD ONTO SMALL PIECES OF TOAST.

Serves **4**
Preparation time **6 minutes**
Cooking time **17 minutes**

Four 5-oz turkey breast steaks
20 unpeeled garlic cloves
1½ cups chanterelle mushrooms,
   lightly rinsed
1¼ cups medium-dry white wine
   or 1¼ cups chicken broth
2 Tbsp balsamic vinegar
A few drops Tabasco Sauce
4 Tbsp sour cream
1 Tbsp chopped fresh flat-leaf parsley

TO SERVE

Triangles of toast, mashed potatoes,
   carrots, wilted spinach tossed with
   fine sliced sautéed mushrooms and
   lemon zest

Wipe the turkey breasts. Lightly brush or spray your grill pan with oil then place on a moderate heat until hot. Add the turkey and seal on both sides for 2 minutes. Press down firmly so the breasts become marked with the ridges of the grill pan.

Lower the heat and add the garlic cloves, mushrooms, and the wine or broth. Simmer for 12 minutes or until the turkey is done. Remove the turkey, garlic cloves, and mushrooms from the pan, place on a warm serving plate, and keep warm.

If the sauce has reduced considerably, add a further 3 to 4 tablespoons of wine or broth. Add the vinegar and Tabasco Sauce to taste and cook for 1 minute before adding the sour cream.

Carefully swirl or stir the juices until blended then pour over the turkey and sprinkle with the chopped parsley. Serve with triangles of toast, on which to spread the softened garlic, with the mashed potatoes, and the carrot, spinach, and mushroom mixture.

Southern Chicken

SOUTHERN CHICKEN

THIS CLASSIC FRIED CHICKEN DISH WORKS WELL IN A GRILL PAN.

Serves **4**
Preparation time **15 minutes**
Cooking time **21 to 24 minutes**

FOR THE CHICKEN

4 boneless, skinless chicken breasts

2 Tbsp white all-purpose flour

Salt and freshly ground black pepper

1 tsp ground allspice

2 Tbsp chopped fresh thyme or
  2 tsp dried

1 medium egg, beaten

1½ to 2 cups fresh white bread crumbs

2 Tbsp sunflower oil

1 Tbsp butter

FOR THE FRITTERS

1 medium egg, beaten

6 Tbsp milk

¾ cup white all-purpose flour

1 cup canned corn kernels, drained

4 scallions, trimmed and chopped fine

1 Tbsp chopped fresh thyme

1 Tbsp oil

TO GARNISH

Fresh parsley sprigs

TO SERVE

Wedges of corn bread

Wipe the chicken breasts, make three diagonal slashes across each, and set aside. Mix the flour with the seasoning, allspice, and thyme, then use to coat the chicken.

Place the egg and bread crumbs in two separate bowls then dip the chicken first in the egg then coat with the bread crumbs.

Lightly brush or spray your grill pan with oil then place on a moderate heat until hot. Add the oil and butter and heat until melted. Add the chicken and cook for 15 to 17 minutes, turning at least once, or until done. Remove and keep warm.

Meanwhile make the fritters by mixing the egg and milk into the flour to form a thick batter. Stir in the drained corn, scallions, and thyme.

Add the oil to the pan then cook the fritters in the pan for 4 to 5 minutes, turning once, until golden. Remove from the pan and keep warm.

Garnish and serve the chicken and fritters with corn bread if using.

SILKEN CHICKEN KABOBS

MARINATING THE CHICKEN IN THE YOGURT MAKES IT VERY TENDER. IF YOUR GRILL PAN IS NOT A NONSTICK ONE YOU MAY NEED A LITTLE EXTRA OIL WHEN COOKING AND DO ENSURE THAT THE PAN IS HOT.

Serves **4**
Preparation time **8 to 10 minutes plus**
  30 minutes marinating time
Cooking time **6 to 8 minutes**

1 lb boneless, skinless chicken
A few strands saffron
½ cup low-fat, plain yogurt
5 to 6 green cardamom pods, lightly
  crushed
2 cinnamon sticks, lightly crushed
2 stalks lemon grass (outer leaves
  removed), chopped fine
2 Tbsp chopped fresh cilantro

TO GARNISH
Lemon wedges

TO SERVE
Warm naan bread and pappadams,
  Yogurt and Cucumber Dip (see page
  17), and red onion salad

Cut the chicken into thin strips and place in a shallow dish. Infuse the saffron in 1 tablespoon of hot water for 5 minutes, then stir into the yogurt. Add the cardamom pods, cinnamon sticks, and chopped lemon grass and pour over the chicken. Cover and leave for 30 minutes in the refrigerator, stirring occasionally.

Drain the chicken, and thread onto eight small wooden skewers (if using lemon grass stalks instead of skewers it is easier if you pierce the chicken first).

Lightly brush or spray your grill pan with oil then place on a moderate heat until hot. Cook the chicken for 6 to 8 minutes, turning frequently, or until done.

Sprinkle with the chopped cilantro, garnish with the lemon wedges, and serve with the bread, pappadams, Yogurt Dip, and salad.

Turkey Mole Kabobs

TURKEY MOLE KABOBS

THE COMBINATION OF CHOCOLATE AND MEAT IS TYPICAL OF
MEXICAN CUISINE AND WORKS VERY SUCCESSFULLY.

Serves **4**
Preparation time **15 minutes plus**
 20 minutes rehydrating time and
 30 minutes marinating time
Cooking time **20 to 22 minutes**

3 to 4 dried ancho chillies or 1 to 2 tsp
 crushed dried chilies, to taste
1 Tbsp oil
1 small onion, peeled and fine chopped
3 garlic cloves, peeled and crushed
8 oz ripe tomatoes, peeled and chopped
1 Tbsp tomato paste
⅔ cup broth
1 tsp ground cinnamon

½ tsp ground cloves
1 oz semisweet chocolate
2 Tbsp chopped fresh cilantro
1 lb fresh turkey breast
2 Tbsp toasted sesame seeds

TO GARNISH
Lime wedges

TO SERVE
Freshly cooked rice with chopped
 fresh cilantro stirred in; tomato
 salsa; and avocado, tomato, and sliced
 onion salad

If using dried chillies rehydrate in hot water for 20 minutes. Heat the oil in a small
pan and sauté the chillies, onion, and garlic for 5 minutes. Add the tomatoes, the
tomato paste blended with the broth, and the spices.

Simmer for 10 minutes, add the chocolate, and stir until melted. Stir in the chopped
cilantro then allow the sauce to cool.

Slice the turkey into thin strips and place in a shallow dish and pour over the
cooled sauce. Cover and leave in the refrigerator for 30 minutes, spooning the
marinade occasionally over the turkey. When ready to cook, drain the turkey, and
thread onto eight skewers.

Lightly brush or spray your grill pan with oil then place on a moderate heat until
hot. Cook the kabobs for 5 to 7 minutes, turning frequently, or until the turkey is
thoroughly cooked. Remove from the pan and sprinkle with the sesame seeds.
Serve on a bed of cooked rice, garnished with lime wedges, with the salsa and salad.

CHICKEN AND TARRAGON BURGERS

THESE BURGERS MAKE A SOPHISTICATED ALTERNATIVE TO ORDINARY BURGERS AND ARE IDEAL FOR AN INFORMAL LUNCH OR SUPPER PARTY.

Place all the ingredients for the burgers except the Parma ham in a food processor and blend for 1 minute or until the mixture forms a ball. Remove from the processor bowl and, with dampened hands, shape into four burgers.

Lightly cover and leave in the refrigerator for 30 minutes. Remove from the refrigerator and wrap two slices of Parma ham around each burger.

Lightly brush or spray your grill pan with oil then place on a moderate heat until hot. Cook the burgers for 5 to 6 minutes each side or until done. Remove and keep warm.

Split the buns or rolls in half and place cut-side down in the grill pan for 2 minutes or until heated.

Place on serving plates, top with arugula leaves, a cooked chicken burger, onion slices, and a spoonful of relish. Serve immediately with fries and coleslaw.

Serves **4**
Preparation time **6 minutes**
  plus 30 minutes chilling time
Cooking time **12 to 14 minutes**

1¼ lbs fresh ground chicken
6 scallions, trimmed and chopped
  fine
¼ cup toasted pine nuts
2 Tbsp chopped fresh tarragon
1 Tbsp paprika
1 Tbsp fine grated lemon zest
Salt and freshly ground black
  pepper
8 slices Parma ham

TO SERVE

4 burger buns or ciabatta rolls;
  rinsed arugula leaves; 1 red
  onion, peeled and sliced thin;
  assorted relishes; large fries;
  and coleslaw

TURKEY WITH ASPARAGUS SPEARS

IF YOU WISH TO SERVE A SAUCE WITH THIS DISH, A RED WINE SAUCE WOULD GO VERY WELL.

Serves **4**
Preparation time
  12 to 15 minutes
Cooking time **12 to 15 minutes**

1 lb fresh asparagus
Four 4-oz turkey escalopes
2 Tbsp cranberry sauce
3 oz feta cheese, sliced into
  4 sticks
A few fresh chervil sprigs
8 Canadian bacon slices

TO GARNISH
Chervil sprigs

TO SERVE
**Mashed potatoes mixed with
  crisp cooked chopped bacon;
  the remaining asparagus,
  heated; and cranberry sauce**

Blanch the asparagus in boiling water for 5 minutes. Drain and refresh in cold water. Place the escalopes between two sheets of waxed paper and pound with a meat mallet until ¼ inch thick. Spread with the cranberry sauce then place two to three asparagus spears on top with a slice of feta cheese and chervil sprigs.

Roll up then wrap two slices of bacon round each, securing with fine twine or toothpicks.

Lightly brush or spray your grill pan with oil then place on a moderate heat until hot. Cook the turkey in the pan for 12 to 15 minutes, turning occasionally, or until done.

Drain, slice, and garnish with chervil sprigs. Serve on a bed of mashed potatoes with bacon, the remaining asparagus, and cranberry sauce.

TURKEY YAKITORI

THESE DELICIOUS, TENDER KABOBS CAN BE SERVED HOT OR COLD. WHEN SKEWERING THEM DO NOT PUSH THE MEAT TOO CLOSE TOGETHER OR THE TURKEY WILL TAKE LONGER TO COOK.

Serves **4**
Preparation time
  **8 to 10 minutes plus
  30 minutes marinating time**
Cooking time **8 to 10 minutes**

1 lb turkey breast
2 Tbsp sake or sherry
2 Tbsp light soy sauce
1 Tbsp dark soy sauce
2 Tbsp orange juice
1 Tbsp soft brown sugar

FOR THE DIPPING SAUCE
2 Tbsp light soy sauce
4 Tbsp orange juice
**2 scallions, trimmed and
  chopped fine**
**1 small chili, seeded and
  chopped fine**

TO GARNISH
Orange wedges

TO SERVE
**Steamed rice, grated daikon
  (Japanese radish), and Oriental
  Salad (see page 102)**

Cut the turkey into thin strips and place in a shallow dish. Blend together the sake or sherry, soy sauces, orange juice, and sugar and pour over the turkey. Cover lightly and leave in the refrigerator for 30 minutes, spooning the marinade occasionally over the turkey. When ready to cook, drain and thread onto eight small wooden skewers.

Meanwhile combine all the ingredients for the dipping sauce in a bowl and set aside, to allow the flavors to develop.

Lightly brush or spray your grill pan with oil then place on a moderate heat until hot. Cook the kabobs for 8 to 10 minutes, turning frequently, or until the turkey is done. Garnish and serve with the dipping sauce and the rice, daikon, and salad.

TURKEY WITH RED PESTO

THERE ARE MANY VARIATIONS ON THE CLASSIC PESTO, WHICH IS MADE WITH BASIL, GARLIC, PINE NUTS, OLIVE OIL, AND PARMESAN CHEESE. THIS VERSION USES SUN-DRIED TOMATOES, BUT TRY USING WALNUTS, PECANS, OR TOASTED HAZELNUTS AND REPLACE THE TRADITIONAL BASIL WITH ARUGULA, WATERCRESS, OR PARSLEY OR A MIXTURE OF FRESH HERBS OF YOUR CHOICE.

Finely chop the tomatoes and place in the food processor with the parsley, pine nuts, and Parmesan cheese. Blend for 1 minute then, with the motor still running, slowly add the olive oil until a thick spreadable consistency is formed.

Wipe the turkey and place between two sheets of waxed paper. Pound to a thickness of ¼ inch with a meat mallet. Place on a chopping board and spread with the prepared pesto.

Cut the Gruyère into four sticks and place on the turkey then roll up. Wrap the bacon around the turkey rolls and secure with toothpicks or fine twine.

Lightly brush or spray your grill pan with oil then place on a moderate heat until hot. Cook the turkey rolls, turning frequently, for 16 to 18 minutes or until done. Remove and keep warm. Add the onion and cook for 5 minutes. Remove and add to the turkey.

Pour the wine into the pan, bring to a boil and boil for 5 minutes or until reduced by about half. Add the honey with the cream and simmer for 2 minutes, carefully swirling or stirring until blended. Return the turkey and onion to the pan and heat for 2 minutes.

Slice the turkey rolls and arrange on warm serving plates, drizzle with the sauce, garnish with parsley, and serve with the noodles and ratatouille.

Serves **4**
Preparation time **15 minutes**
Cooking time **30 to 32 minutes**

FOR THE PESTO
2 Tbsp semidried or sun-dried tomatoes
2 Tbsp flat-leaf parsley
2 Tbsp toasted pine nuts
½ cup grated Parmesan cheese
3 Tbsp olive oil

FOR THE TURKEY
Four 4-oz turkey breast steaks
One 4-oz piece Gruyère cheese
8 bacon slices
1 large red onion, peeled and sliced thin
1¼ cups medium-dry white wine
2 tsp liquid honey
4 Tbsp heavy cream

TO GARNISH
Fresh flat-leaf parsley sprigs

TO SERVE
Freshly cooked noodles tossed in butter and chopped parsley, and ratatouille

CHICKEN AND CORN WITH PESTO

CUT THE WING TIPS OFF THE CHICKEN WINGS SO THAT THEY WILL SIT PROPERLY IN THE GRILL PAN
AND BE THOROUGHLY COOKED.

Wipe the chicken wings and place in a shallow dish. Place the basil, garlic, pine nuts, and honey in a food processor. Blend for 1 minute then with the motor still running slowly pour in the oil. Scrape into a bowl and stir in the Parmesan cheese. Use to brush over the chicken wings. Thread onto eight skewers and refrigerate until required.

Remove the silky threads from the corn cobs then pull up the outer leaves and loosely tie with fine twine.

Boil the sweet potatoes in lightly salted boiling water for 3 minutes or until almost tender, drain, and set aside.

Lightly brush or spray your grill pan with oil then place on a moderate heat until hot. Add the corn on the cob and cook for 15 to 20 minutes, turning occasionally, until tender. Remove from the pan and wrap in foil to keep warm. If the corn cobs do not have all their outer leaves, remove the leaves and silky threads, cook in gently simmering water for 10 minutes, drain well and cook in the grill pan for 5 to 7 minutes, turning frequently.

Add the skewered wings to the pan and cook for 15 to 20 minutes or until done. The juices should run clear, not pink, when the wings are pierced with a knife. Remove and keep warm.

Wipe the pan clean and add the sunflower oil. Cook the potato slices for 3 to 4 minutes, or until tender and golden, turning at least once.

Serve the chicken wings sitting on the sweet potatoes, with the corn on the cob and the tomato salad and garnished with the herbs.

Serves **4**
Preparation time **10 minutes plus 30 minutes marinating time**
Cooking time **37 to 47 minutes**

12 to 16 chicken wings, depending on size

½ cup fresh basil leaves

2 garlic cloves, peeled and crushed

2 Tbsp pine nuts

1 Tbsp liquid honey

4 Tbsp olive oil

2 Tbsp grated Parmesan cheese

4 small corn on the cob, outer leaves retained

1½ lb sweet potatoes, peeled and sliced thick

2 to 3 Tbsp sunflower oil

TO GARNISH
Fresh herbs

TO SERVE
Tomato salad

VEGETABLES

ORIENTAL SALAD

YOU CAN USE WHATEVER ORIENTAL SALAD VEGETABLES ARE AVAILABLE FOR THIS DISH BUT REMEMBER THAT
BEAN SPROUTS HAVE A VERY SHORT SHELF LIFE SO DO NOT BUY UNTIL YOU ARE ACTUALLY GOING TO USE THEM.

Lightly brush or spray your grill pan with oil then place on a
moderate heat until hot.

Cut the bell peppers into quarters and seed. Place skin-side
down in the hot grill pan and cook for 10 minutes or until the
skins have blistered. Remove from the pan, place in a plastic
bag, and allow to cool. Peel off the skins and finely shred the
bell peppers.

Place the water chestnuts, bok choi, scallions, bean sprouts,
and daikon or radishes in a bowl and add the bell pepper strips.

Heat the dressing ingredients in the grill pan until hot, pour
over the salad, toss, and serve sprinkled with the cilantro.

Serves **4 to 6**
Preparation time **12 minutes**
Cooking time **10 minutes**

1 red and 1 yellow bell pepper
1 cup canned water chestnuts,
   drained and cut in half
3 small bok choi heads, rinsed
   and shredded
8 scallions, trimmed and sliced
   diagonally
2 cups bean sprouts
One 4-oz daikon (Japanese
   radish), peeled and grated or 1
   small bunch radishes, trimmed
   and sliced
2 Tbsp chopped fresh cilantro

FOR THE DRESSING
1 Tbsp sherry or sake
2 Tbsp light soy sauce
1 to 2 tsp liquid honey
2 Tbsp sunflower oil

CHARGRILLED VEGETABLES WITH GREEN OLIVES

THIS DISH IS IDEAL SERVED ON ITS OWN WITH PLENTY OF WARM CRUSTY BREAD OR AS A SIDE DISH.

Place the olives, capers, oil, lemon zest, and juice in a food processor and blend to a purée. Season with the black pepper and set aside.

Cut the bell peppers, zucchini, and onions into bite-size pieces and place in a shallow dish. Cut the garlic cloves in half and add to the vegetables. Pour over the olive purée, stir, and leave in the refrigerator for 30 minutes, stirring occasionally.

Lightly brush or spray your grill pan with oil then place on a moderate heat until hot. Drain the vegetables then cook in the pan for 15 to 20 minutes or until done and the vegetables have begun to char slightly. You may need to cook the vegetables in two batches. Sprinkle with the basil and serve with the polenta.

Serves **4**

Preparation time

8 to 10 minutes plus 30 minutes marinating time

Cooking time **15 to 20 minutes**

¾ cup green olives, pitted

1 Tbsp capers

5 Tbsp olive oil

1 Tbsp grated lemon zest

3 Tbsp lemon juice

Freshly ground black pepper

3 bell peppers in assorted colors, seeded

2 medium zucchini, trimmed

2 medium onions, peeled

4 garlic cloves, peeled

TO GARNISH

2 Tbsp chopped fresh basil

TO SERVE

Pan-grilled polenta wedges to serve

(see page 104)

VEGETABLE POLENTA TRIANGLES

INSTANT POLENTA IS VERY EASY TO USE. WITH SOME GRATED PARMESAN CHEESE STIRRED IN, IT MAKES A GOOD ALTERNATIVE TO RICE, PASTA, OR POTATOES.

Bring 3¾ cups water to a boil in a large saucepan, add the polenta with seasoning to taste, and mix until smooth. Cook over a gentle heat, stirring for 5 minutes or until the polenta is thick. Spoon into a lightly oiled 7-inch square pan and allow to cool. When cold cut into triangles.

Meanwhile place the vegetables in a large shallow dish and pour over the olive oil and lemon juice. Cover and leave for 30 minutes in the refrigerator, occasionally stirring the vegetables.

Lightly brush or spray your grill pan with oil then place on a moderate heat until hot. Drain the vegetables, reserving 2 to 3 tablespoons of the marinade, and cook in the pan for 15 minutes or until done, turning the vegetables as they char. (You may need to do this in two batches, depending on the size of your grill pan.) Remove from the pan and keep warm.

Add 1 tablespoon of the marinade to the pan then add the polenta triangles to the hot pan and cook for 4 minutes each side or until piping hot. (You may need to cook the polenta in two batches, adding the remaining marinade.)

Serve the polenta with the vegetables, scatter with the basil sprigs and shavings of Parmesan cheese.

Serves **4**
Preparation time **10 minutes plus 30 minutes marinating time**
Cooking time **28 minutes**

1½ cups polenta
Salt and freshly ground black pepper
3 bell peppers in assorted colors, seeded and cut into thick strips
1 large onion, peeled and cut into wedges
4 to 6 garlic cloves, peeled and sliced in half
3 cups field mushrooms, wiped and sliced
6 Tbsp olive oil
3 Tbsp lemon juice

TO GARNISH
A few fresh basil sprigs

TO SERVE
Shavings of Parmesan cheese

CHARGRILLED MEDITERRANEAN
VEGETABLES

BELL PEPPERS, EGGPLANTS, AND ZUCCHINI ARE VERY FLAVORFUL WHEN CHARGRILLED IN THE GRILL PAN.

Serves **4**
Preparation time **12 to 15 minutes**
Cooking time **21 minutes**

2 red bell peppers, seeded and sliced
1 small eggplant, trimmed and cubed
1 zucchini, trimmed and cubed
6 to 8 shallots, peeled and cut in half
6 unpeeled garlic cloves
4 Tbsp olive oil
3 plum tomatoes
2 Tbsp red wine vinegar
1 Tbsp balsamic vinegar

TO GARNISH
Fresh basil leaves and freshly ground black pepper

Lightly brush or spray your grill pan with oil then place on a moderate heat until hot. Add the bell peppers, eggplant, zucchini, shallots, and garlic with 2 tablespoons of the oil and cook, stirring occasionally, for 15 minutes or until the skins are beginning to char.

Cut the tomatoes in halves or quarters, depending on size, add to the pan, and continue to cook for 5 minutes or until the vegetables are tender. Pour over the remaining oil, red wine vinegar, and balsamic vinegar, heat for 1 minute, then serve sprinkled with the basil and pepper.

POLENTA AND PEPPER SQUARES

MAKE THE POLENTA AHEAD OF TIME, COVER, AND STORE IN THE REFRIGERATOR UNTIL YOU ARE READY TO SERVE IT.

Serves **4**
Preparation time **15 to 18 minutes**
Cooking time **23 minutes**

4 Tbsp olive oil
1 medium red onion, peeled and chopped fine
2 garlic cloves, peeled and crushed
1 red and 1 green bell pepper, skinned *(see page 110)*, seeded, and chopped fine
1 tsp crushed dried chillies
1½ cups polenta
Salt and freshly ground black pepper
½ cup grated Parmesan cheese
4½ cups wild and button mushrooms, wiped and sliced if large

TO GARNISH
Shavings of Parmesan cheese and chopped flat-leaf parsley

Heat 1 tablespoon of the oil in the grill pan and sauté the onion and garlic for 5 minutes or until softened, remove from the heat, and stir in the chopped red and green bell peppers and the crushed chillies.

Bring 3¾ cups water to a boil in a large saucepan, add the polenta with seasoning to taste, and mix until smooth. Stir in the Parmesan cheese then cook over a gentle heat, stirring, for 5 minutes or until the polenta is thick. Stir in the cooked onion and pepper mixture.

Spoon into a lightly oiled 7-inch square pan and allow to cool. When cold cut into squares.

Lightly brush or spray your grill pan with oil then place on a moderate heat until hot. Add 1 tablespoon of the oil to the pan and cook the polenta in two batches, adding a further tablespoon of oil, for 4 minutes each side or until piping hot. Keep warm.

Heat the remaining oil in the grill pan and sauté the mushrooms for 5 minutes, stirring constantly. Arrange the cooked polenta on serving plates, top with the lightly cooked mushrooms, and scatter with the Parmesan and parsley.

SWEET POTATO AND
GARBANZO BURGERS

THESE ARE IDEAL TO SERVE AT A PARTY, WHERE SOME OF THE GUESTS MAY BE VEGETARIAN. MAKE THEM BITE-SIZE.

Cook the sweet potatoes in lightly salted boiling water for 12 minutes or until soft. Drain, mash well, and set aside.

Drain the garbanzos and blend in a food processor until a coarse-textured purée is formed. Add to the mashed potatoes.

Heat 1 tablespoon of the oil in a small pan and sauté the onion, garlic, and chillies for 5 minutes or until softened. Remove from the heat and stir into the potato and garbanzo mixture. Season to taste and stir in the chopped cilantro. Add enough flour to make a stiff consistency.

Shape into four burgers on a lightly floured board and lightly coat in flour. Cover lightly and chill in the refrigerator for at least 30 minutes, or longer, if time permits.

Lightly brush or spray your grill pan with oil then place on a moderate heat until hot. Add 1 tablespoon of the oil and cook the burgers in the pan for 3 minutes each side, adding the extra oil when the burgers are turned over.

Place four tomato slices on top of each burger, add a slice of cheese, and cook for a further 1 to 3 minutes or until burgers are piping hot and the cheese has begun to melt. Remove and keep warm.

Toast the split buns in the grill pan for 1 to 2 minutes then remove from the pan. Cover the buns with salad leaves, add the burgers, and top with either mayonnaise or salsa. Close the buns and serve.

Serves **4**
Preparation time **8 to 10 minutes plus 30 minutes chilling time**
Cooking time **25 to 27 minutes**

10 oz sweet potatoes, peeled and cut into small pieces

2 cups canned garbanzos

3 Tbsp sunflower oil

1 small onion, peeled and chopped fine

3 garlic cloves, peeled and crushed

2 red jalapeño chillies, seeded and chopped

Salt and freshly ground black pepper

2 Tbsp chopped fresh cilantro

3 to 4 Tbsp white all-purpose flour

4 oz Fontina or Gruyère cheese, sliced thin

4 tomatoes, sliced

4 buns, split in half

TO SERVE

Salad leaves, mayonnaise or red chili salsa

BABY EGGPLANT WITH
GOAT CHEESE

IF BABY EGGPLANTS ARE UNAVAILABLE USE ONE SLICED LARGE EGGPLANT INSTEAD.
THE RECIPE WILL WORK JUST AS WELL.

Trim the eggplants, cut in half, and place in a shallow dish. Blend the oil, garlic, lemon juice, and zest and pour over the eggplants. Scatter with the basil. Cover and leave in the refrigerator to marinate for 30 minutes. Spoon the marinade over occasionally.

Lightly brush or spray your grill pan with oil then place on a moderate heat until hot. Drain the eggplants, reserving a little of the marinade, and cook in the grill pan for 8 to 10 minutes or until just done, occasionally turning the eggplants over.

Cut the goat cheese into thin slices and place a slice on each eggplant half. Spoon over a little of the reserved marinade.

Continue to cook for a further 2 to 3 minutes or until the goat cheese begins to melt. Serve immediately, scattered with more chopped basil if liked, with the bread and salad.

Serves **4**
Preparation time **5 to 8 minutes plus**
  30 minutes marinating time
Cooking time **10 to 13 minutes**

8 small baby eggplants, lightly rinsed
8 Tbsp olive oil
4 garlic cloves, peeled and crushed
4 Tbsp lemon juice
1 Tbsp grated lemon zest
2 Tbsp chopped basil
8 oz goat cheese in a roll

TO GARNISH
Chopped basil, optional

TO SERVE
Warm crusty bread and salad

GRAPE LEAF AND HAVARTI PARCELS

THESE DELICIOUS PARCELS MAKE A WONDERFUL APPETIZER OR LIGHT LUNCH FOR TWO OR THREE PEOPLE.

Lightly brush or spray your grill pan with oil then place on a moderate heat until hot.

Cut the bell peppers into quarters and seed. Place skin-side down in the hot grill pan and cook for 10 minutes or until the skins have blistered. Remove from the pan, place in a plastic bag, and allow to cool. When cool, peel off the skins and cut the bell peppers into strips.

Meanwhile place the grape leaves in a bowl, pour over boiling water, and leave for 20 minutes. Drain and rinse well in fresh water then pat dry.

Cut the scallions into strips of a similar length to the pepper strips. Cut the cheese into eight to ten equal pieces.

Spread the grape leaves out on a chopping board and divide the bell peppers, scallions, and cheese on top. Scatter with the chili and cilantro and season with the black pepper.

Roll up and secure with fine twine or toothpicks. (To ensure that the filling is properly encased, you may find it necessary to use two grape leaves per parcel.)

Lightly brush or spray your grill pan with oil then place on a moderate heat until hot. Add the sunflower oil and, when it is hot, cook the parcels for 4 to 6 minutes or until hot and the cheese is beginning to melt. If using twine, discard and pierce the parcels with toothpicks.

Serve immediately, garnished with lemon wedges and black olives. If serving as a light lunch, serve on a bed of assorted salad leaves, with cherry tomatoes, and crusty bread.

Serves **2 to 3**
Preparation time **12 to 14 minutes plus 20 minutes soaking time**
Cooking time **14 to 16 minutes**

1 red and 1 yellow bell pepper
16 to 20 small grape leaves
8 scallions, trimmed
8 oz havarti cheese
1 red jalapeño chili, seeded and chopped
2 Tbsp chopped fresh cilantro
Freshly ground black pepper
1 Tbsp sunflower oil

TO GARNISH
Lemon wedges and black olives

TO SERVE
Assorted salad leaves, cherry tomatoes, and crusty bread

RED BEAN AND RICE FALAFEL

A VARIETY OF BEANS CAN BE USED FOR THESE. TRY CANNELLINI, GARBANZOS, OR BORLOTTI BEANS OR EVEN A COMBINATION OF TWO OR THREE.

Serves **4**
Preparation time **10 minutes**
Cooking time **7 to 10 minutes**

2 cups canned red kidney beans,
   drained and rinsed
1 small onion, peeled and chopped
3 garlic cloves, peeled and crushed
1 jalapeño chili, seeded and chopped
½ cup cashew nuts, chopped
2 Tbsp chopped fresh cilantro

1 cup freshly cooked basmati rice
1 medium egg yolk
1 to 2 Tbsp white all-purpose flour
2 Tbsp sunflower oil

TO SERVE
4 large pita breads; shredded iceberg
   lettuce; 8 scallions, trimmed and
   shredded; tomato salsa; or ½ cup
   Monterey Jack cheese, grated; 4 to 6
   Tbsp Garlic Mayo *(see page 113)*

Place the beans, onion, garlic, chili, cashew nuts, and cilantro in a food processor and blend for 1 minute. Add the rice and blend again for a further minute. Add the egg yolk and blend for 1 to 2 minutes or until the mixture comes together.

Turn out onto a lightly floured board and shape into 2-inch long oval shapes. Coat in the flour, place on a plate, and chill for 30 minutes. When ready to cook, carefully thread two or three falafel onto eight small wooden skewers.

Lightly brush or spray your grill pan with oil then place on a moderate heat until hot. Add 1 tablespoon of sunflower oil and cook the falafel for 6 to 8 minutes, turning frequently or until piping hot. Add the extra oil as the pan becomes dry. Remove and keep warm.

Heat the pita bread in the grill pan for 1 to 2 minutes. Remove and split in half. Place shredded lettuce in the pita breads and top with the shredded scallions.

Take the falafel off the skewers, place on top of the scallions, and top with salsa; alternatively, place a spoonful of the Garlic Mayonnaise on top and sprinkle with grated cheese.

Red Bean and Rice Falafel

SWEET POTATO WITH GARLIC MAYO

MAKE THE GARLIC MAYONNAISE ON THE DAY YOU ARE SERVING IT AND REFRIGERATE BEFORE USE.

Serves **4**
Preparation time **8 minutes plus 30 minutes marinating time**
Cooking time **23 minutes (for two batches)**

1½ lb sweet potatoes, peeled and sliced
6 Tbsp olive oil
3 garlic cloves, peeled and crushed
1 tsp crushed chillies
2 Tbsp butter

FOR THE GARLIC MAYO

2 medium egg yolks *(see page 4)*
2 garlic cloves, peeled and crushed
Salt and freshly ground black pepper
1 tsp Dijon mustard
3 Tbsp lemon juice
1¼ cups olive oil
1 Tbsp chopped fresh parsley

Cook the potatoes in lightly salted boiling water for 2 minutes, drain, and return to the heat. Cover with the lid and shake the pan so the potato slices are dried then place in a shallow dish. Blend 4 tablespoons of oil, garlic, and chillies and pour over the potatoes. Cover and leave in the refrigerator for 30 minutes.

Meanwhile make the mayonnaise by placing the egg yolks, garlic, seasoning, mustard, and lemon juice in a food processor and blend for 30 seconds. With the motor still running, slowly pour in the olive oil until the mixture is thick and emulsified. (Add a little extra lemon juice or hot water if the mayonnaise is too thick.) Scrape into a bowl, stir in the parsley, and leave in the refrigerator until required.

Lightly brush or spray your grill pan with oil then place on a moderate heat until hot. Add the butter and remaining oil and allow to melt, then add the potato slices (do this in two batches). Cook for 10 minutes, turning the slices over at least once until golden, crisp, and done. Serve with the mayonnaise.

SPICED COUSCOUS SALAD

COUSCOUS IS EXTREMELY EASY TO PREPARE AND COMBINES WELL WITH MANY DIFFERENT FLAVORS.

Serves **4**
Preparation time
 8 to 10 minutes
Cooking time **10 minutes**

1 red and 1 yellow bell pepper
1½ cups couscous
A few saffron strands
½ to 1 tsp dried crushed chillies
1 tsp ground cumin
1 tsp ground coriander
½ tsp ground ginger
½ small cucumber, chopped
**6 scallions, trimmed and
  chopped fine**
2 Tbsp chopped fresh cilantro
3 Tbsp olive oil
2 Tbsp lemon juice

Lightly brush or spray your grill pan with oil then place on a moderate heat until hot.

Cut the bell peppers into quarters and seed. Place skin-side down in the hot grill pan and cook for 10 minutes or until the skins have blistered, pressing them down lightly in the pan. Remove from the pan, place in a plastic bag, and allow to cool. Peel off the skins and chop the bell peppers.

Cover the couscous with about 2½ cups boiling water, sprinkle in the saffron, and leave until all the water is absorbed, stirring occasionally with a fork. Stir in the remaining spices with the chopped cucumber, scallions, and chopped cilantro. Blend together the oil and lemon juice, pour over the couscous, stir thoroughly until well mixed, and serve.

BEAN BURGERS

YOU CAN USE A VARIETY OF BEANS FOR THESE, BUT TRY TO INCLUDE RED KIDNEY BEANS FOR FLAVOR AND COLOR.

Serves **4**
Preparation time **5 minutes**
 plus 30 minutes chilling time
Cooking time **6 to 8 minutes**

**2 cups canned red kidney beans,
  drained and rinsed**
**1¼ cups canned flageolet beans,
  drained and rinsed**
**3 garlic cloves, peeled and
  crushed**
**1 medium onion, peeled and
  chopped**
1 tsp ground coriander
1 tsp ground cumin
1 tsp turmeric

**Freshly ground black pepper
  to taste**
**¼ cup fresh whole wheat bread
  crumbs**
2 Tbsp chopped fresh cilantro
1 medium egg, beaten

TO GARNISH

Fresh herbs and lemon slices

TO SERVE

**Sautéed sweet potatoes and
  Waldorf salad**

Place all the ingredients for the burgers in a food processor and process for 1 to 2 minutes or until well blended. Scrape out of the bowl and with dampened hands form into four burgers. Place on a plate, cover lightly, and chill in the refrigerator for 30 minutes.

Lightly brush or spray your grill pan with oil then place on a moderate heat until hot. Cook the burgers for 3 to 4 minutes each side or until done and piping hot.

Garnish with the herbs and lemon and serve with the sweet potatoes and salad.

DESSERTS

RUM-FLAMBÉED PINEAPPLE

THE PINEAPPLE FOR THIS RECIPE MUST BE RIPE. THE BEST
WAY TO TEST FOR RIPENESS IS TO ENSURE THAT THE PINEAPPLE
HAS A STRONG PINEAPPLE AROMA THEN PULL OUT ONE OF
THE LEAVES FROM THE PLUME—IF IT COMES OUT EASILY THE
PINEAPPLE IS RIPE.

Serves **4**
Preparation time **10 to 12 minutes**
Cooking time **6 minutes**

⅔ **cup heavy cream**
2 **Tbsp orange-flower water**
1 **large ripe pineapple**
½ **stick sweet butter**
¼ **cup light soft brown sugar**
5 **Tbsp dark rum**
1 **Tbsp grated orange zest**
2 **Tbsp crystallized ginger, chopped**
2 **Tbsp toasted slivered almonds**

TO DECORATE
1 **Tbsp confectioner's sugar, sifted**

Whip the cream until soft peaks form and stir in the orange-flower water. Cover
and chill in the refrigerator until required.

Discard the plume from the pineapple and cut away the peel. Cut into rings and,
using a small cutter, cut out and discard the hard central core. Pat dry with
paper towels.

Lightly brush or spray your grill pan with oil and place on a moderate heat until
hot. Add the butter and when melted, stir in the sugar. Take off the heat and
carefully swirl the pan (or stir) until the sugar has melted. Return the pan to the
heat, add the pineapple, and cook for 2 minutes each side.

Pour in the rum, heat for 1 minute, then remove from the heat and carefully set alight.
When the flames have subsided, add the orange zest, ginger, and almonds, heat
briefly then serve, sprinkled with the confectioner's sugar, with the flavored cream.

Rum-flambéed Pineapple

BANANAS WITH CINNAMON
MASCARPONE

WHEN MAKING PRALINE, ADD A LITTLE WATER WHEN
DISSOLVING THE SUGAR. IT SPEEDS UP THE PROCESS AND ALSO
ENSURES THAT THE SUGAR THOROUGHLY DISSOLVES WITH NO
DANGER OF BURNING.

Serves **4**
Preparation time **15 minutes**
Cooking time **14 to 16 minutes**

½ cup sugar

½ cup whole almonds, shelled

1¼ cups mascarpone cheese

1 to 1½ tsp ground cinnamon

2 to 3 Tbsp light cream or low-fat, plain
   yogurt

4 medium ripe but firm bananas

2 to 4 Tbsp dark soft brown sugar

Lightly oil a baking sheet and set aside. Place the sugar in a heavy-based
saucepan with 2 tablespoons of water and heat gently, stirring occasionally until
the sugar has melted. Bring to a boil and boil vigorously for 5 minutes or until a
light caramel is formed. Add the almonds then remove from the heat and pour
immediately onto the oiled baking sheet. Allow to cool. When cold break into
small pieces with a meat mallet or rolling pin. Store in an airtight container if not
using immediately.

Cream the mascarpone cheese with cinnamon to taste then beat in the cream or
yogurt until smooth. Add the praline and set aside.

Lightly brush or spray your grill pan with oil then place on a moderate heat
until hot. Add the unpeeled bananas and cook for 6 to 8 minutes or until the
skins have blackened. Remove from the heat, carefully split open the skins, and
sprinkle with the brown sugar. Serve with spoonfuls of the cinnamon-flavored
mascarpone cheese.

CALVADOS APPLES

CALVADOS IS A FINE APPLE BRANDY MADE IN NORMANDY, NORTHERN FRANCE, WITH A DISTINCTIVE FLAVOR OF RIPE APPLES. IF CALVADOS IS UNAVAILABLE USE A GOOD-QUALITY BRANDY.

Beat ¾ stick of butter with the sugar until creamy then slowly add the Calvados, beating well after each addition. Set aside the remaining butter. Place in a small serving bowl and refrigerate for 1 hour or until firm.

Peel the apples, core, and cut into slices. Toss in the lemon juice and set aside.

Lightly brush or spray your grill pan with oil then place on a moderate heat until hot. Add the remaining butter and draw the pan off the heat until the butter has melted. Carefully swirl the pan until the butter coats the base, then add the apple slices and cook for 2 to 3 minutes each side or until the apples have begun to caramelize.

Scatter with the lemon zest and serve warm, drizzled with maple syrup, and with spoonfuls of the Calvados butter and cookies.

Serves **4**
Preparation time **5 to 8 minutes plus 1 hour chilling time**
Cooking time **4 to 6 minutes**

1 stick sweet butter
½ cup light soft brown sugar
3 to 4 Tbsp Calvados brandy
4 medium apples
2 Tbsp lemon juice

TO DECORATE
Lemon zest and maple syrup

TO SERVE
Cookies

WARM BANANAS WITH
CHOCOLATE CREAM

THE CHOCOLATE CREAM IN THIS RECIPE CAN ALSO BE USED AS
A FILLING FOR SMALL PASTRY CASES OR A CAKE.

Serves **4**
Preparation time **5 minutes plus**
   2 hours chilling time
Cooking time **10 to 12 minutes**

4 oz semisweet chocolate
1 to 2 Tbsp dark soft brown sugar
⅔ cup heavy cream
2 Tbsp brandy
4 medium bananas

TO SERVE

Mascarpone cheese, 4 to 6 Tbsp
   freshly squeezed orange juice, 1 Tbsp
   grated orange zest, 2 Tbsp toasted
   slivered almonds

Break the chocolate into small pieces and place in a heavy-based pan with the
sugar, cream, and brandy. Heat gently, stirring occasionally until the chocolate
has melted. Remove from the heat and stir until smooth and free from lumps.

Pour into a bowl, allow to cool, then leave in the refrigerator for about 2 hours
or until firm. Remove and whisk until light and fluffy. Set aside.

Lightly brush or spray your grill pan with oil then place on a moderate heat until
hot. Add the unpeeled bananas and cook for 6 to 8 minutes or until the skins
have blackened.

To serve, scrape out the cooked bananas and mash the flesh with the orange
juice. Gently mix with the chocolate sauce and mascarpone cheese to give a
rippled effect and pile into serving glasses. Sprinkle with orange zest and the
toasted slivered almonds.

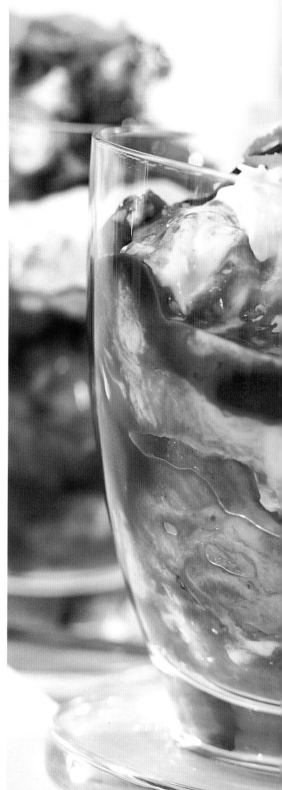

Warm Bananas with Chocolate Cream

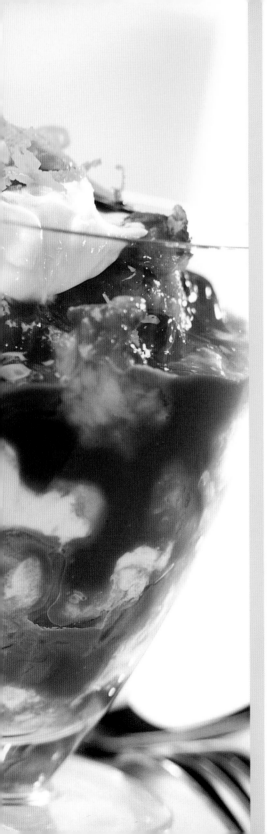

ROQUEFORT PEARS WITH HAZELNUTS

THE PEARS USED IN THIS RECIPE NEED TO BE FIRM BUT JUST BEGINNING TO RIPEN. AVOID USING PEARS THAT ARE OVERRIPE. IF LIKED, ANY OTHER GOOD-QUALITY BLUE CHEESE CAN REPLACE THE ROQUEFORT.

Serves **4**
Preparation time **5 to 8 minutes plus 30 minutes chilling time**
Cooking time **6 to 8 minutes**

3 oz Roquefort cheese
4 Tbsp sour cream
3 Tbsp whole shelled hazelnuts
4 ripe but firm pears
2 Tbsp lemon juice
¾ stick sweet butter
4 slices panettone (Italian sweet bread)

Cream the cheese with the sour cream until smooth, cover, and refrigerate for at least 30 minutes.

Lightly brush or spray your grill pan with oil then place on a moderate heat until hot. Add the hazelnuts and cook for 2 to 3 minutes, stirring frequently until toasted. Remove, cool, and chop.

Peel, halve, and core the pears, then brush with the lemon juice.

Lightly brush or spray the grill pan again with a fine mist of oil and reheat. Add 4 tablespoons of the butter, draw off the heat, and carefully swirl the pan until the butter has melted.

Toast the panettone for 1 minute on both sides then remove from the pan and set aside.

Add the remaining butter to the pan, swirl gently, then add the pear halves, hollow-side down into the pan and cook for 2 to 3 minutes or until lightly charred.

Remove the pears from the pan and place small spoonfuls of the creamed cheese in the hollows. Sprinkle with the chopped hazelnuts and serve on the toasted panettone with any remaining cheese mixture.

FRUIT AND MARSHMALLOW KABOBS

THE COMBINATION OF THE WARM MANGO AND MELTING MARSHMALLOWS IS IRRESISTIBLE.

Heat the sugar, ½ stick of butter, and corn syrup in a heavy-based pan until blended, stirring occasionally. Remove from the heat and stir in the cream. Stir well then pour into a serving jug and refrigerate for at least 30 minutes.

Prepare the fruits, lightly rinsing any that do not need to be peeled, and cut into bite-size pieces. Thread onto eight small wooden skewers with the marshmallows.

Lightly brush or spray your grill pan with oil and place on a moderate heat until hot. Add the 3 tablespoons of butter, remove from the heat, and carefully swirl the pan until melted. (If using fruit bread, toast the bread for 1 minute each side, remove, and set aside.)

Add the skewers and cook, turning occasionally, for 1 to 2 minutes or until the marshmallows are toasted.

Serve sitting on the toasted bread with the chilled toffee sauce and decorate with mint sprigs and spoonfuls of mascarpone or cream.

Serves **4**
Preparation time **8 to 10 minutes**
 plus 30 minutes chilling time
Cooking time **8 to 10 minutes**

½ **cup dark soft brown sugar**
½ **stick sweet butter**
2 Tbsp corn syrup
⅔ **cup light cream**
10 oz assorted fresh fruits,
 such as papaya, mango, melon,
 apple, and strawberries

18 marshmallows
3 Tbsp sweet butter
4 slices fruit bread (optional)

TO DECORATE
Mint springs

TO SERVE
Mascarpone cheese or lightly
 whipped heavy cream

PINEAPPLE KABOBS WITH
MAPLE SYRUP

IF LIKED, THREAD THE SKEWERS WITH OTHER PIECES OF FRUIT
AS WELL AS THE PINEAPPLE. TRY STRAWBERRIES, GRAPES,
ORANGE SEGMENTS, OR APPLE WEDGES.

Serves **4**
Preparation time **8 minutes plus
  15 to 30 minutes standing time**
Cooking time **6 to 8 minutes**

1 large pineapple
1 to 2 tsp ground ginger
5 Tbsp maple syrup
¼ cup orange juice
2 Tbsp crystallized ginger

TO DECORATE
1 Tbsp confectioner's sugar, sifted

TO SERVE
Chocolate ice cream

Discard the plume from the pineapple, cut away the skin, slice, and remove the
hard central core. Cut into small pieces and thread onto eight small wooden
skewers then sprinkle with the ground ginger. Allow to stand for 15 to 30 minutes.

Lightly brush or spray the grill pan with oil then place on a moderate heat until
hot. Add the pineapple skewers to the pan and heat for 1 minute. Pour over
the maple syrup and cook for 3 to 5 minutes, turning occasionally, until hot.
Remove from the pan and place on serving plates.

Add the orange juice and crystallized ginger to the grill pan and bring to a boil.
Boil for 2 minutes then carefully pour over the pineapple.

Sprinkle with the confectioner's sugar and serve with spoonfuls of chocolate
ice cream.

Melon Medley

MELON MEDLEY

THIS IS AN EXTREMELY ATTRACTIVE DESSERT TO SERVE AT A DINNER PARTY. FOR MAXIMUM EFFECT, USE A VARIETY OF DIFFERENT COLORED MELONS.

Serves **6 to 8**
Preparation time **10 minutes**
Cooking time **4 minutes**

**¾ cup fresh or defrosted frozen
 raspberries**
2 Tbsp lemon juice
2 Tbsp confectioner's sugar, or to taste
**3 small assorted colored melons (or use
 3 large wedges)**
½ stick sweet butter

TO DECORATE
Extra raspberries

TO SERVE
Cookies (optional)

Place the raspberries in the bowl of the food processor with the lemon juice and sugar and blend for 1 minute. Pass through a fine sieve to remove the pips, pour into a serving jug, and set aside.

Cut the melon into wedges, remove from the skin, and discard the seeds. Cut into small wedge-shaped slices.

Lightly brush or spray your grill pan with oil then place on a moderate heat until hot. Add the butter then remove from the heat and carefully swirl the pan until melted.

Add the melon slices and cook for 2 minutes each side then arrange on serving plates. Pour a little of the raspberry coulis around and decorate with extra raspberries. Serve with cookies if using.

WARM PAPAYA AND
MANGO SALAD

THIS EXOTIC SALAD IS A TRUE TASTE OF THE CARIBBEAN. A PERFECT TREAT AFTER
A DAY AT THE BEACH.

Blend the coconut milk with the superfine sugar until soft
then gradually blend in the vanilla extract. Spoon into a
small serving bowl, sprinkle with half the raw brown sugar,
and set aside.

Peel the mangos and papayas, discarding the pit and seeds,
and slice fairly thickly.

Lightly brush or spray your grill pan with oil then place on
a moderate heat until hot. Add the butter, draw off the heat,
and carefully swirl until the butter has melted.

Return to the heat and add the sliced fruit. Cook for 5 minutes
or until the fruit is lightly caramelized.

Sprinkle with the remaining raw brown sugar and rum, heat
for 1 minute, then arrange on serving plates. Serve the
coconut milk as a dipping sauce.

Serves **4 to 6**
Preparation time **8 to 10 minutes**
Cooking time **6 minutes**

1 cup coconut milk
1 Tbsp superfine sugar
½ tsp vanilla extract
4 Tbsp raw brown sugar
1 large or 2 small mangos
1 large or 2 small papayas
½ stick sweet butter
2 to 3 Tbsp dark rum

INDEX